To John,

Happy 75th.

Love,

Sue

September, 2007
Donegal

Donegal
South of the Gap

Paintings by Brian Gallagher
Stories by Liam Ronayne

First published by Cottage Publications,
Donaghadee, N. Ireland 2000.
Copyrights Reserved.
© Illustrations by Brian Gallagher 2000.
© Text by Liam Ronayne 2000.
All rights reserved.
No part of this book may be reproduced or
stored on any media without the express
written permission of the publishers.
Design & origination in Northern Ireland.
Printed & bound in Singapore.

ISBN 1 900935 15 5

The Author

This is Liam Ronayne's second book in the series, following the publication of *Donegal Highlands* in 1998. His interest in history began as a boy growing up in East Cork, and was further stimulated by his history teacher at secondary school in Fermoy. A graduate in law (National University, Cork) Liam has been Donegal County Librarian since 1984.

Liam was joint editor, with Willie Nolan and Mairead Dunlevy, of *Donegal: history and society; interdisciplinary essays on the history of an Irish county*, published by Geography Publications in 1995, a major history of the county from the earliest times. Other publications include articles on Donegal's workhouses, and on a variety of bibliographical and information science topics. He is on the editorial board of the County Donegal Historical Society's journal, the *Donegal Annual*, to which he contributes a guide to Donegal local studies each year. He is currently editing a booklet on the Battle of Scariffholis, the 350th anniversary of which occurs in 2000.

The Artist

Brian Gallagher was born in Newcastle upon Tyne, England. However his father was from Gortahork in Northwest Donegal and, having spent many long holidays there, Brian soon developed strong ties to the County.

At college Brian studied Art and Design, going on to obtain a BA(hons) degree in Illustration / Graphics at Bristol. After graduation he began his career as a free lance Illustrator based in London and worked for many magazine, newspaper and book publishers such as The Evening Standard, The Observer, Harper Collins and Longmans amongst others.

Now living and working in Dublin as a full time artist, his work predominantly features scenes of Co. Donegal. Using acrylics he attempts to capture the power and excitement of the rugged earth and sky. His illustration work continues with a number of Irish clients such as the Bar Review and Business Plus. He exhibits widely and his work can be viewed at a number of galleries around Ireland.

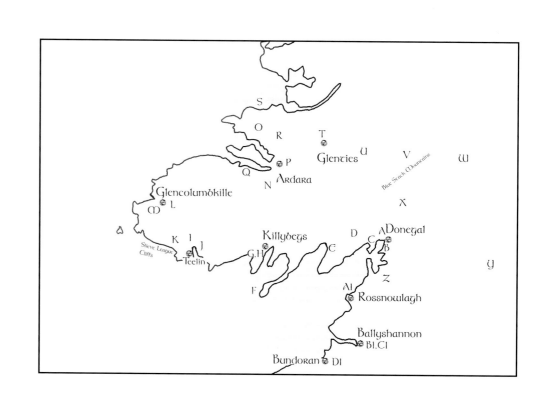

S

O
R   T
                Glenties U   V   W
P
Q
N   Ardara   Blue Stack Mountains

Glencolumbkille
M   L   X

                                                    A Donegal
K I   Killybegs   D   C
Slieve League   J   C   B
Cliffs   G,H   C
Teelin   Z

                                     A1   Y
F   Rossnowlagh

                                  Ballyshannon
                                  B1,C1

Bundoran D1

Contents

Beginnings

Those intrepid Victorian travellers Mr. and Mrs. Samuel Carter Hall wrote, "Unequalled in Ireland for wild and rude magnificence" when they visited Donegal in 1840. Their *Tour of Ireland*, published the following year, went on to say

"From the immense proportion of waste land in county Donegal the reader may form some idea of the barren aspect of the county, and, at the same time, of its surpassing beauty"

This judgement on what Donegal has to offer the tourist has been repeated by many travellers since, yet it has always reflected only half the story. South and Southwest Donegal contains mountains, bogs, and rough land, and more than its share of natural beauty, but it has also seen the mark of man - it has ancient monuments, castles, monasteries, well kept farms, and busy little towns, as well as Ireland's leading fishing port.

The Hall's book devotes fewer pages to County Donegal than it does to Louth, Ireland's smallest county, but this lack of interest in the County was by no means unique. Donegal saw fewer eighteenth and nineteenth century visitors than other parts of the country - neither the immense sea cliffs of Sliabh a'Liag (Slieve League), nor the Poisoned Glen drew the visitor in the same numbers as did the Lakes of Killarney, the Wicklow Mountains, or the Glens of Antrim. In part this was because Donegal was seen as comparably inaccessible even then, and in turn it contributed to Donegal remaining perhaps Ireland's least known major county. When the visitors did come they tended to visit mainly the south of the county, often on their way to Enniskillen or Derry.

If the county was neglected by travellers in the past, one has to say that local correspondents did not always present their area in the best possible light. For instance a landowner from the Pettigo district wrote in the 1820s, in response to a query from the North West of Ireland Farming Society

"meagre and dry to the last degree must appear the description of a region where the hand of nature, severely parsimonious, has been very niggardly aided by the ingenuity of art or the tasteful design of scientific industry".

Beginnings

He did add

"beautiful indeed and picturesque in many places the scenery must appear to the eye of a poet"

but even this was qualified by the view that

"when considered in an agricultural, commercial or manufacturing point of view, it presents a spectacle little fitted to captivate the fancy of the theoretical or invite the labours of the practical improver".

A colleague of his, John Ewing, gave this description of Gleann Cholm Cille or Glencolumbkille

"no modern buildings, no towns, no gentlemen's seats; the scenery an alternate succession of rocks, mountains and improvable valleys; no inn. Roads horribly bad: not a perch of good road in the parish".

It must be remembered that Ewing was writing about an area immeasurably rich in folklore and folk ways, one that in the native tradition was a place to be envied. With such a gap in comprehension between well-intentioned men like him and the Gaelic speaking inhabitants it is perhaps no surprise that 17th and 18th century attempts at 'improvements' had such mixed results.

Developments in technology hold out the promise that many young people will in time get to look at the world from space; this may still be some time off but even looking at a satellite photo of the south of the County one quickly sees how well defined the area is. South and Southwest Donegal, the area covered by this book, looks like a somewhat mis-shapen horseshoe stretching around Donegal Bay. It is defined on its southern edge by the Bay which washes the shore from Sliabh a'Liag to Bundoran, and by the Croaghs or Bluestack mountains which act as a granite boundary to the north, ending in Barnesmore (the "Great Gap") the gateway between North and South Donegal, and indeed between the west and north of Ireland. The massive Sliabh a'Liag peninsula with its huge sea cliffs closes the area off on the west, while the Gweebarra river acts as its boundary with the Rosses and Northwest Donegal.

County Donegal as a whole comprises an area of 1,193,621 acres, equivalent to 483,042 hectares. Less than half, in fact only some 400,000 acres, is suitable for agriculture. Almost twice that amount consists of rough pasture and upland bog 600 feet or more above sea level, and where it is used at all it is mainly for sheep grazing. More than 24,000 acres are under water, including lakes and major tidal inlets. While the southwest of the county contains extensive areas of rough pasture and upland bog as well as many lakes and inlets, the land in the barony of Tirhugh is good farming land. This fertile area on either side of where the River Eske enters Donegal Bay at Donegal Town and southwards to the river Erne has been farmed since the early historic period, although archaeological evidence suggests that it was not settled in the Neolithic and Early Bronze Age era, perhaps because it was so extensively forested at the time. The eastern edge of South Donegal surrounding Lough Derg and adjoining Fermanagh has many small lakes. Lough Derg has long been a centre of pilgrimage, and in medieval times was the only place in Ireland which most Europeans would have heard of. It is easy to see why people believed that this barren area, with its thin blanket bog covering metasedimentary rocks, led to the gates of Purgatory.

Although original forests have almost entirely vanished, as late as the early 1600s there was significant afforestation, especially in the south of the County. In her study of the woodlands of Donegal, Dr. Eileen McCracken found that the area around Donegal Bay from Ballintra west to Killybegs was covered by trees, as was the area between Ardara, Glenties and Narin. In from the coast, the River Eske valley up to Lough Eske and the area to the west of Lough Derg were also heavily forested.

One of the distinctive features of the Donegal Town area is the preponderance of drumlins. These are tightly compacted and rounded mounds of boulder clay and sand and gravel, formed by glacial drift 10,000 - 12,000 years ago. Druimlín means a "little ridge or back' and is the term applied to these hillocks usually between 60 and 100 metres high, although some are a little higher. The drumlins around Donegal Bay are part of a chain which extends across Ireland from here to Strangford Lough on the County Down coast; this drumlin belt has been a barrier to communication since prehistoric times and has acted as a cultural barrier for most of that time, being in effect the boundary between Ulster to the north and Connacht and Leinster to the south. The swarms of drumlins around Donegal Town - along the eastern shore of Donegal Bay down to Rossnowlagh, and westwards as far as Bruckless - are the dominant feature of the landscape; they dictate the pattern of roads and fields, even to the present day, while the rivers, like the Eske, the Drummenny and the Eany Water have to negotiate their way around them to flow into the Bay.

Donegal is acknowledged as one of the most complex areas in Ireland in terms of its geology. Geologists will tell you that if the history of the earth is a book, the Precambrian era makes up the first chapter. Human beings are not unnaturally concerned with their own place in history, so it is more than a little sobering to observe that the Precambrian era is not a foreword or preamble but the longest chapter, some 88% of geologic time in fact. It runs from the beginning of the planet itself, some 4.5 billion years ago, right to the Cambrian period, just over half a billion years ago. The Precambrian was the era of microscopic life, predating not only humans and other mammals, but dinosaurs and even snails. Microscopic life, creepy crawlies too small to see and get upset about, may not be to everyone's taste, but scientists are sure that we would not be here without them.

The landscape of Donegal has such a look of permanence that one has to struggle to accept that it was formed at a time when the planet was already old. It is not easy for the layperson to grasp just how long ago these processes happened, or the violent movement that was involved.

Four hundred million years ago Donegal and Northwest Europe was subject to a period of sustained earth movement. The earth's plates were at that time moving towards each other, bringing Europe and North America together and in the process squeezing the Atlantic. This movement forced the rocks to fold up like cardboard and led to the creation of an immense mountain chain stretching all the way from Scandinavia through Scotland, the Northwest of Ireland, the North Atlantic, to Newfoundland off the coast of what is today Canada. Because this folding of rocks to form mountains was first described in Scotland, the mountains so formed are known as Caledonian, from the Roman name for Scotland. In Donegal the most obvious results of this

movement are the fault lines running northeast to southwest, for example those at Glenveagh, in the northwest of the county and at Barnesmore the gateway from North to South Donegal.

One result of the formation of the Donegal mountains was that rocks were put under unimaginable stress, making them molten and merging them with older rocks. These igneous rocks - from the Latin word for fire - are one of the main types of rocks in Donegal and elsewhere. The granite which was formed in this way and which is so associated with Barnesmore and elsewhere in Donegal, dates from this era. Granite is not the only kind of rock found in Donegal, as the area has plenty of examples of metamorphic rocks as well. Metamorphic rocks are those which have been changed by heat, and you will see signs of faults and folding. Schists and gneisses are typical metamorphic rocks. Schist - schistus means easily cleaved in Latin - is fairly easy to break up, in contrast to both granite and quartzite. Quartzite is a sandstone that has been changed into hard quartz.

As recently as ten thousand years ago Donegal was covered in ice. The ice was not static, however, but moving towards the sea, bringing with it rough gravel which had an effect rather like giant sandpaper on the rocks, leaving them smoother and more rounded than before. In some places the movement of the ice led to deep and distinctive scores on the rocks, which allow us today to see the direction of the iceflow. The Croaghs or Blue Stack mountains were scraped bare in this way, with the debris being left in the valleys below. The indented coastline, and the sea cliffs at Sliabh a'Liag and Malainn Mór (Malinmore) were shaped by erosion, which is still occurring. Glaciation and the movement of huge sheets of ice across the landscape thus had a huge influence on how South Donegal looks today; in particular it caused the scouring of the huge U-shaped valleys of Barnesmore and Glengesh.

Global warming is much in the news these days, but in fact the earth has never been in an unchanging state; our world is always either getting warmer or cooler, drier or wetter, but at such a slow rate that it is hardly noticeable. When the glacial age ended and the ice retreated the valleys and lower slopes of the hills came to be covered in trees, mostly pine and birch. Around 6,000 BC Ireland's climate was entering a colder and damper period, resulting in much of the country being waterlogged, lack of drainage being a feature of glaciated areas. Forests and low lying land became marshes, but did not become lakes. Instead the partly decomposing trees and other plants formed peat bogs. In Gleann Cholm Cille (Glencolumbkille) there are extensive areas of blanket bog, much of them protected by law as repositories of a unique ecology, home to insect animal and plant life which evolved there and which are not to be found in more fertile areas. The Pettigo and Lough Derg area also has extensive blanket bogs.

These bogs were vital to the inhabitants of the glen and other similar areas, and continue to provide a valuable fuel. Saving the turf was an important feature, a ritual even, of the year's work, involving the entire community, and continues today despite modern pressures. The time to cut the turf is just when the bog has begun to dry out but before it dries out too much, leaving the sod hardened. This is usually in late April or May. The central importance of turf cutting to the local way of life is illustrated by the way in which Gaelic terms live on in everyday usage. The turf banks are known in the glen as bachtaí, which are prepared each year by slicing off the scraith or top sod. The tool used all over the country for cutting the turf is known as the sleán, a long bladed spade - no English term for this tool has ever caught on - while the reek of dried turf outside the house is known as a clampar. Pleasant though a summer's day can be out on the bog, with hot tea and thick slices of bread for the hungry workers, the turf cutters have to put up with the míoltógaí or midges, which can try the patience of the most even-tempered.

Just as glaciation and millennia of climatic phenomena have shaped the landscape, so the landscape has shaped the people who live in South and Southwest Donegal, as the rest of this book hopes to show.

When Sir Henry Sidney, the Lord Deputy of Ireland, first set eyes on the O'Donnell castle at Donegal in 1566 he found it

"one of the greatest that ever I saw in any Irishman's lands, and would appear in good keeping one of the fairest . ."

Sidney's visit came less than a decade into the Elizabethan age, and at a time when the O'Donnells' power was unchallenged in the Northwest of Ireland. The Castle had been built sixty years earlier, by Aodh Ruadh (Hugh Roe) Ó Domhnaill, the second chieftain to bear that name. The first Aodh Ruadh had built the Friary just outside the town in 1474 for the Franciscan Order.

The castle remained the centre of O'Donnell power for a century, a period which saw great change in Ireland. It was only when the Tudors took the business of conquest seriously that the power of the great Ulster chieftains began to wane; as O'Donnell power ebbed at the beginning of the seventeenth century, the castle was taken over by the English, just a couple of years before the death of Elizabeth I. The castle was appropriated by Captain Basil Brooke in 1611.

Brooke was knighted in 1616, and he proceeded to convert the building into a Jacobean residence. He first transformed the tower, the taller part of the complex, into a comfortable home, adding gables and windows, and creating a banqueting room on the first floor, where the famous Brooke fireplace signified the family's arrival as powerful landowners. He then added the manor house at right angles to the tower, and built a gate tower as the main entrance to the old O'Donnell bawn, the area around the castle.

Dúchas~the Heritage Service has recently completed a programme of repair and refurbishment, and an hour or two in the castle gives the modern visitor an idea of the style in which the new elite created by the Ulster Plantation lived.

Donegal Castle

BRIAN GALLAGHER '99

When, in the Autumn of 1585, the authorities in Dublin Castle were 'shiring' the western parts of the province of Ulster, i.e. dividing it up into counties, they faced a dilemma in naming the westernmost part. The name they chose was not Tirconnel, the English version of Tír Chonaill which was the name used by the local people; instead they called the county after the key town at the head of the bay which divides - or joins - Connacht and Ulster. In the opinion of the officials

"the towne of Donnygall is the only place for her majestie's gaole and sheere towne, for her highnes' cessions and jaile deliverie, within the said countye of Donnygall"

That this spot had long been an important one is clear from the annals and from the derivation of the placename itself. While the name had no territorial application before 1585, its adoption by the authorities meant that it soon replaced Tirconnell for administrative and legal purposes, although Tír Chonaill is still used by Gaelic speakers, and until recently by such bodies as the GAA. The first record of a placename in the area is in 1289, when an Anglo-Norman document refers to Thethnegall (Teach na nGall or 'house of the foreigners'). *The Annals of the Four Masters* refer to a place called Áth na nGall ('the ford of the foreigners') in 1419. It is more than probable that Teach na nGall, Áth na nGall and Dún na nGall all refer to the same place. There is no certainty about which 'foreigners' built the settlement here; the Normans were in Tír Chonaill for at least half a century before the document of 1289, but all the evidence points to the place being named sometime after the ninth century. If this is the case the foreigners were more than likely to have been Vikings.

Donegal Town continues to be the main centre of the south of the county. Here in the Diamond, the three-sided square in the heart of the town, three important roads meet: the road to Ballyshannon, Sligo and the south, the road heading to Letterkenny, Lifford and Derry, as well as that leading to Ireland's premier fishing port at Killybegs. The town was also a hub in the era of rail travel, when three County Donegal Railway lines met there - from Ballyshannon, from Killybegs, and from Stranorlar, from which there were connections to Glenties, Strabane, Letterkenny, and Derry.

Donegal Town

BRIAN GALLAGHER '00

Just outside the town of Donegal, in the townland of Magherabeg, are the ruins of a monastery that has a special place in Irish history. The building of the Friary for the Franciscan Order began in 1473 or 1474, under the patronage of Aodh Ruadh I Ó Domhnaill and his wife Nuala O'Brien. It quickly became a flourishing religious centre, and the burial ground of the Tír Chonaill nobility, earning a very special place in the heart of all the O'Donnell chieftains.

It was not immune, however, from the troubles of the times. Sir Henry Sidney, whom we have already met at Donegal Castle, noted in 1566 that the friary would be "with small cost very forticable". Twenty two years later, in 1588, most of the friars fled when South Donegal was under attack from a raiding party sent by Dublin Castle. The guardian, Tadhg Ó Baoighill, stayed behind thinking that he would be safe, but was killed by soldiers entering the Friary, and found in the doorway by the friars on their return. The Friary had, needless to say, been plundered. Three years later the friary was again attacked and garrisoned, but the soldiers were driven out by Aodh Ruadh II Ó Domhnaill in 1592. In 1601 the monastery was under attack again, this time by a party of English led by the renegade Niall Garbh Ó Domhnaill. During the siege the building was blown up and the subsequent fire left it a ruin. Although some attempts to repair it were made before it came into the hands of the Brookes, it served only as a burial ground until comparatively recent times.

After the destruction of Donegal Friary, the focus of the Franciscans in the county seems to have shifted to their house at Bundrowes, near Bundoran. It was here, in January 1632, that Brother Michéal Ó Cléirigh and his fellow Franciscans Cúchoigriche Ó Cléirigh, Fearfeasa Ó Maolchonaire (from Roscommon) and Cúchoigriche Ó Duibhgheannain (from Leitrim) began work on what was to become the most important record of Irish history until modern times. Originally, and properly, called *Annála Rioghachta Éireann*, the *Annals of the Kingdom of Ireland*, it was first called the *Annals of the Four Masters*, in honour of the four Franciscans who compiled it, by fellow seventeenth century cleric John Colgan. The *Annals* are undoubtedly the greatest legacy of the Donegal friars.

Donegal Friary

BRIAN GALLAGHER '00

Mountcharles is some four miles west of Donegal Town on the road to Killybegs. It looks down over the shore of Donegal Bay. This little town of Mountcharles will forever be associated with the writer Seumas Mac Manus.

Mac Manus was born in Mountcharles, and used to sit at the pump at the western end of the town in his later years, telling stories and entertaining the local children. Mac Manus published a huge number of books - stories, poetry and plays - most of it based on the stories that he had heard as a youngster. The titles of some of his most popular books - *In chimney corners: Irish folk tales, The Donegal wonder book, Donegal fairy stories, The Humours of Donegal, 'Twas in Dhroll Donegal* - give a fair idea of their content. Mac Manus was very popular in the United States amongst both Irish immigrants and Irish Americans, and spent much of his adult life on that side of the Atlantic.

He met and fell in love with Anna Johnston, a young woman from County Antrim who was involved in cultural nationalist circles, and they married in 1901. She died the following year, while still a young woman, but left behind a small body of poetry under the nom de plume Ethna Carbery, which many consider to be more interesting than Mac Manus' own work.

Mac Manus also played a large part in founding the Gaelic Athletic Association in County Donegal. At his urging a meeting was held on 23rd October 1905 in MacIntyre's Commercial Hotel, Mountcharles - known at the time as 'Cassie Mac's' - to establish a Donegal County Board of the GAA. Association football had already put down strong roots in Donegal at the time, perhaps because of the county's links with the West of Scotland, and the formation of a county board happened much later than in many other counties. South and Southwest Donegal is still the stronghold of Gaelic Football, and no fewer than 12 of the 15 who started in the Donegal team in their triumphant All-Ireland Final in September 1992 were from clubs in the south and southwest.

Mountcharles

BRIAN GALLAGHER '00

The ruined church at Killaghtee and the graveyard which surrounds it are located just outside Dunkineely on the road to St. John's Point. There is not much to see nowadays of the church ruins, and the place is, as a local writer remarked, one hundred and thirty years ago, "principally remarkable for the immense number of ponderous tombstones which meet the visitor at every step". The site overlooks the sea, just a little ways to the southwest.

The church was originally built in the twelfth century, the parish church of Killaghtee, and was in use until 1826 when the present Church of Ireland parish church was built in Dunkineely. The east gable and part of the south wall are all that remain, and even these are covered by the heavy growth. Killaghtee churchyard is mainly visited, when it is visited at all, because of the interesting standing stone, called by archaeologists a cross-inscribed slab. The historian of early Irish art Francoise Henry dated it to the second half of the seventh century, and saw it as a stage in the evolution between inscribed stones and the much better known Celtic crosses. One of the remarkable features of the Killaghtee slab is the Celtic three-cornered knot, known as a triquetra, which apparently represents the Trinity.

As we have seen, the churchyard is full of tombstones. Not all of them are from ancient times, never mind the seventh century; one poignant reminder of more recent times is the headstone of a Canadian airman whose body was washed ashore near here during World War II.

A little further down from Killaghtee churchyard towards St. John's Point, and looking out over the sea are the ruins of McSwyne's castle at Rahan. This was the seat of power of the Mac Suibhne Boghaineach, the Sweeney Banagh. The Mac Suibhne Boghaineach were one of the three branches of the powerful Sweeney clan, and controlled a huge swaythe of territory in the southwest from the fourteenth century until the Ulster Plantation. Their chieftains controlled the sea trade from their castle on this promontory, as well as the land from the Eany Water which flows into the sea at Inver to the Dobhair River, the northern boundary of the Rosses.

Killaghtee

BRIAN GALLAGHER '00.

The Lighthouse at St. John's Point provides a vital service to the fishermen of Southwest Donegal, along with its sister lighthouses on Rathlin O'Beirne Island and on Rotten Island at the entrance to Killybegs harbour.

The lighthouses of the Irish coast have been automated for some years, but Kinnfaela (T. C. McGinley) in his book *The Cliff-scenery of south-western Donegal* published in 1867, gives us an entertaining account of what it was like to visit here in a more gracious era. Having arrived at the St. John's Point Lighthouse he tells us that "we need not be backward in ringing the bell, for Mr. Brunelle is exceedingly courteous to visitors"; he then enters

"the front yard, beautifully paved with fine brown sandstone, and kept at all times scrupulously clean. In this yard stands the lighthouse, a lofty circular tower, with a balcony round it near the top, and roofed in dome-like form. The walls near the top supporting the dome consist of large plates of glass, through which the blaze from the reflectors within are transmitted in all directions".

St. John's Point is the most southerly part of Southwest Donegal and from the precincts of the Lighthouse on even a halfway decent day one can take in all that Donegal Bay has to offer. To the south is the coastline of Sligo and North Mayo, with the island of Inishmurray, rich in archaeological remains, and Streedagh Point where the Spanish Armada came to grief. Looking north one can see right into Killybegs Harbour, and watch the modern trawlers, Irish and foreign-owned, making their way to and from Ireland's premier fishing port. To the west the coastline ends in the massive sea cliffs of Sliabh a'Liag, and to the east one can see past Doorin Point towards Donegal Town at the head of the Bay. Immediately below the Lighhouse the land ends in a fork, with a narrow inlet known as Fox's Hole in between. It would be hard to better Kinnfaela's description of a stormy day here, when

"the wind blows strongly from the south, it is a grand sight to behold the foaming swell of the surges, as they dash up the storm-beaten rocks, and break into the finest dust-like spray".

St. John's Point

BRIAN CALLAGHER '99

Spend a little while in Killybegs and you will soon agree that the townspeople are proud of their status as Ireland's leading fishing port. There is much more to Killybegs than the fishing however; it is a town with a long and interesting history in its own right.

When the County Donegal Railways line reached here in 1893, a visiting journalist noted that

"Rome is built on seven hills, but Killybegs is built on seven hundred hills"

The area around the deep fjord-like inlet of Killybegs has been inhabited since prehistoric times, as evidenced by the twenty or more ring forts that remain, most of them near the shore. The town was named in early Christian times, the name Na Cealla Beaga referring to a group of monastic cells. Interestingly, and perhaps surprisingly in a region not short of native saints, the town's patron saint is St. Catherine of Alexandria. That this St. Catherine is the patron of seafarers surely confirms that Killybeg's tradition of seafaring is very old indeed.

The Mac Suibhne Boghaineach (Sweeney Banagh) were the leading family in medieval times, having displaced the O'Boyles when they carved out the territory for themselves in the late middle ages. While their main seat was in the castle of Rahan, near Dunkineely, Killybegs was their main port.

In the Autumn of 1588 Killybegs hoved into the centre of European history, when the remains of the Spanish Armada struggled into the harbour on the way home from their doomed attempt to invade England. Three ships made it as far as the bay, most notably the 'Girona'. This galliass - a ship of more than one deck, with two or more banks of oars and two or more masts - was "sore bruised by the seas", and was repaired using timbers from another of the Armada ships which had run aground and broken up off Killybegs. The crews of other ships which were driven ashore in Donegal also made it to Killybegs, leaving the greater part of five ships crews in the town. When the 'Girona' set sail after her repairs with between 1,100 and 1,300 men on board there were still around 2,400 Spaniards in Killybegs. The 'Girona' struck rocks off the Antrim coast, and sank, with only five survivors. The fate of the other 2,400 remains something of a mystery, but one that might have its explanation in the cosmopolitan feel of present day Killybegs.

Killybegs

Killybegs' pre-eminence as a fishing port is not recent. When the O'Donnell chieftains were known as the "best lord(s) of fish in Ireland" in the sixteenth century, Killybegs was the chief port of Tír Chonaill. As early as 1556, Spanish ships bought the right to fish off Killybegs following an agreement between Queen Elizabeth and King Philip of Spain, her erstwhile suitor. The English Exchequer earned one thousand pounds per annum for granting the Spanish fleet this right, but it is not clear how much of this money found its way to the people of the town.

The agriculturist Arthur Young visited Killybegs some two centuries later. In 1776, he was taken by Lord Conyngham's agent for a trip along

"the coast where the fisheries are most carried on, particularly Inver Bay, McSwyne's Bay, and Killybegs Bay. The coast is perfectly sawed with bays. The lands are high and bold particularly about Killybegs, where the scenery is exceedingly romantic . . ."

During the nineteenth century the government made several attempts to put the fishing industry on a sounder footing. A commission of enquiry, which heard evidence in Killybegs in January 1836, found that the years from 1822 to 1831 were disastrous for fishing, as the herring shoals failed to appear, although the story improved radically from 1832 on. During the Famine times of the late 1840s, the availability of fish meant that Killybegs did not suffer greatly; in fact there was much greater distress in the area in the 1860s and especially 1880s, when the potato crop failed again. The establishment of the Congested Districts Board in 1891 opened a new chapter in the fishing industry. During the 1890s a new pier was approved for Killybegs, its £10,000 cost being borne jointly by the Board and the Treasury. The Board also invested in new fishing craft and in fish processing. The coming of the railway in the same decade meant that there was a much quicker way of getting the catch to market.

The super trawlers and their crews which can be seen in the harbour, on the fairly rare occasions they are not harvesting the sea, are thus the latest in a long line of seafarers from the town.

Killybegs Harbour

BRIAN GALLAGHER 00

Stop at a spot called Bar a Bhogaidh just above the road from Cill Chartha (Kilcar) to Gleann Cholm Cille and you will have a panoramic view of the little town of An Charraig (Carrick) and the beautiful countryside which surrounds it. To the west of Teelin Bay rise the immense sea cliffs of Sliabh a'Liag, while one can trace both the Owenwee and Glen rivers as they make their way from the high ground into the Bay.

The most prominent sight in the little town which nestles here is the Catholic church of Naomh Columba built in 1862. Before that date local people worshiped at a scalán or mass house, and tradition has it that they brought stones with them on their way to Sunday mass to build the church. Naomh Columba's is the parish church of the area which includes the western end of the Sliabh a'Liag peninsula, including Gleann Cholm Cille and Teileann. An Charraig is a good place to base oneself when touring the area. A trip by boat down Teelin Bay and along the cliffs is a must for visitors, and until 1824 a boat trip was the easiest way to get to An Charraig. It was in that year that the bridge in the middle of the town was built. The building of the bridge was to a large extent the making of the town, as soon after the authorities built a Post Office, an RIC barracks and a Revenue station, thus establishing it as the focus of the peninsula. After Catholic emancipation in 1829 the church authorities followed suit, building the parish church here rather than in the Glen, although the latter spot is far richer in ecclesiastical associations.

It was the Revenue station which brought Ballyshannon born poet William Allingham to work on this stretch of the coast, and it was the view of Sliabh a'Liag from the road outside An Charraig which inspired one of his most famous verses

Up the airy mountain
down the rushy glen,
we daren't go a-hunting
for fear of little men.

An Charraig

CARRICK

BRIAN GALLAGHER 00

The small coastal village of Teileann (or in English Teelin) is perhaps best known for two things: fishing and traditional fiddle music. Indeed the renowned folklore collector Sean Ó hEochaidh who was born here claims that Teileann can be known equally as 'Teileann an Éisc' and 'Teileann an tSeanchais agus an Cheoil' - 'Teelin of the Fish' and 'Teelin of Tradition and Music'. Teileann is some two miles south of An Charraig on an inlet at the eastern end of the Sliabh a'Liag sea cliffs.

The Teileann area has a long history of fishing, although nowadays it is small scale compared to its near neighbour in Killybegs. This was not always the case, for the village has featured in maritime maps since the 1320s, and the *village for herringe and sometymes for salmon in the creek or bay Teelin"* was noted in a document dating from 1608. As recently as 1898 the village was the leading cod fishing port in Ireland, and five years earlier the Coast Guard based in Killybegs noted that the greatest volume of landings in his division was not in Killybegs itself but in Teileann. It is still a centre for inshore fishing and small-scale commercial fishing, but is today better known as a centre for Donegal fiddle music.

At the end of the nineteenth and beginning of the twentieth centuries the music of the Teileann area was said to be basic in style with little rhythmic variation or ornamentation. Local tradition credits the travelling fiddlers of the Doherty and McConnell families for enhancing the local style and repertoire. Greatest amongst their adherents were the Cassidys, the brothers Paddy, Johnnie and Frank and their cousin Con. According to the account of Donegal fiddle music written by Caoimhín Mac Aoidh, the Cassidys "combined to form one of the most incredible forces in Irish music" in the century just ended. The legacy of the Cassidys, and of other local musicians such as Mick McShane, Jimmy Lyons, and Francie and Jimmy Kelly is still honoured, and the visitor will not have to go far to listen to fiddling of the highest quality in this small coastal village.

Teileann
TEELIN

BRIAN GALLAGHER 00

The Sliabh a'Liag peninsula, roughly equivalent to the parishes of Cill Chartha (Kilcar) and An Charraig (Carrick) and the western end of Ardara parish, is a world in itself, home to a unique way of life with a wealth of folklore. Traditional culture lives on, especially singing and fiddle playing. In an area of breathtaking natural beauty, of hills, glens, and sandy beaches - like An Trá Bhán at Malin Beg - the most outstanding feature is undoubtedly Sliabh a'Liag, the mountain which gives its name to the peninsula, and the sea cliffs on its southern side.

The sea cliffs are, as every local will tell you, the highest in Europe, and Sliabh a'Liag itself rises to 595 metres over the roaring sea below. Getting to the cliffs or the mountain is not easy, but on a calm day is certainly worth the effort. Turn south once you cross the bridge in the village of An Charraig and head for Teileann. Turn right after the pier at Teileann and the road takes you towards Bunglass, where it ends at a car park. After that you are on foot. If you are not an experienced hill-walker you may still appreciate just how awesome Sliabh a'Liag mountain and the cliffs are from the nearby spot known as Amharc Mór and the track which leads on towards the mountain. Getting to the top, along the track known, for obvious reasons, as the 'One Man Pass' is strictly for those who know what they are doing, but if you are up to it is an unforgettable experience.

The sea cliffs are some three kilometres long, and show the effects of millennia of Atlantic storms which have crashed against the rock face, shaping them over time.

There is no shortage of folklore about the mountain and the cliffs. One story tells of the holy well at Diseart Aoidh Mhic Bhricne (named for a local saint), now a ruined monastic site overlooking 'One Man Pass', which was renowned for its curative powers for arthritis. A man of 100, who had made the trip to the summit twice before to cure his arthritis, was so tired from his efforts that he said "'Be the livin', Aodh Mac Bricne, if you don't cure me this time, after me coming to you so often, I'll never come near you again."

Sliabh a'Liag
SLIEVE LEAGUE

BRIAN GALLAGHER '99

As the name suggests, this area is inextricably linked with the memory of Donegal's greatest saint, Colm Cille or Columba. There is a local folk tradition that St. Patrick came to Southwest Donegal in the fifth century, on his mission to convert the people of the northern half of Ireland. He was prevented from entering the glen, however, by demons who made the Glen River into a stream of fire, and caused a permanent fog to descend over the entire area. Patrick accepted defeat, but forecast that a better man than he would finish the job. Some 100 years later Colm Cille, who was born near Lough Gartan in the north of the county, approached the glen with his followers. The demons killed one of them - Cearc - thus giving rise to the place-name Srath na Circe. Colm Cille was not a man to take this lying down so he chased the demons into the sea at a place called Screig na nDeamhan (the demons' rocky shore).

Colm Cille is honoured each year in the turas which takes place in the glen on June 9th (the date of his death). A turas is a devotional journey where pilgrims stop for prayer at a number of sites or stations associated with a saint. Examples are found in many parts of Ireland, although few have the status of the Gleann Cholm Cille turas. The Gleann Cholm Cille turas consists of fifteen stations, most of which are on the northern side of the Murlin River. It starts and finishes here at St. Columba's Church of Ireland, the site of the earliest monastic site in the glen, which tradition holds was founded by Colm Cille.

Each station is marked, and a number of them have beautifully decorated stones. It usually takes between three and a half and four hours to complete the turas, which is about three and a half miles or five kilometres long. Pilgrims doing penance walk the turas barefoot. Despite its connection with Colm Cille, the turas has not always found favour with church authorities, as it is generally agreed that it is left over from pre-Christian times. In the last century an attempt was made to ban the practice, but to no avail. The memory of Colm Cille in the glen was, and still is, far too strong.

Turas
Gleann Cholm Cille
GLENCOLUMBKILLE

BRIAN GALLAGHER '99

Gleann Cholm Cille may be at the end of a long road, as far from the big city as one could get, yet it is a thriving centre of culture. Distance from major centres of population, is not, of course, without its drawbacks, and the people of the glen, or 'in-through' people as the inhabitants of Carrick parish are often called, have always had to make special efforts to counter the effects of isolation. No one exemplified those special efforts more than the former Parish Priest, the late James Canon McDyer.

James McDyer was born in 1910 in Kilraine, the same area, incidentally, as Cardinal Patrick O'Donnell. When he came to Gleann Cholm Cille he found a community that seemed to be on its last legs, with no electricity, no public water supply, almost no roads. The area had endured decades of emigration, and those who remained lived on subsistence farming and fishing. A State which had been established to safeguard Gaelic culture looked the other way as one of the most significant examples of that culture was dying. Unwilling to accept such a fate, Fr. McDyer invigorated the local community and helped establish industries based on local resources - weaving, knitting and fish processing, and succeeded in bringing electricity and a water supply to the glen. The Folk Museum (An Clachán), the community hall (Halla Mhuire), and the holiday village will always be associated with him.

Fr. McDyer's work did not die with him, however, as a number of community led initiatives are now thriving. The work of Oideas Gael is especially noteworthy. This forward looking group organises Gaelic language classes in Gleann Cholm Cille each Summer, bringing people from all over Ireland and Europe, and from as far away as Latin America and Japan. Its base at Foras Cultúir Uladh (Ulster Cultural Foundation) is home to courses in archaeology, art and music.

Another interesting initiative is Táipéis Gael, a group of weavers who make tapestries, wall hangings and other high quality crafts based on local traditions. An tIonad Eachtraíochta at Málainn Mhóir is the base for outdoor pursuits, including sea sports and hill walking trips.

Fr. McDyer's dream lives on.

Gleann Cholm Cille
GLENCOLUMBKILLE

BRIAN GALLACHER '99

A book of this nature could hardly ignore the awesome and often forbidding Pass of Glengesh. T. C. McGinley, under the nom de plume 'Kinnfaela' wrote in his *Cliff scenery of south western Donegal*.

"a work professing to treat of the topography of South-Western Donegal would not be complete without some notice of the remarkable valley of Glengesh".

With or without McGinley's admonition, the road through Glengesh is, on a fine day, a highlight of any visit to this part of Donegal. The County has a number of high passes - Barnesmore, the gap that both links and divides the north and south of the county; the smaller Barnesmore between Termon and Creeslough; and the Gap of Mamore in Inishowen to name the better known ones. Glengesh, however, is arguably the most beautiful and evocative of them all. Few would argue with Dinah Mary Craik, who came here in the 1880s and wrote

"one of the sweetest glens I ever saw ... a view which I can still see with shut eyes, and remember as one of the lovely visions that we carry away with us for ever".

The ancient inhabitants would agree certainly, but perhaps only up to a point; they named this place Gleann na Geise (sometimes Gleann Gheise) - the valley of the taboo or prohibition. What was under taboo is not clear but one can safely assume it related to travelling through the glen when the mists were down. This was no small thing, as the path through Glengesh was, and still is, the direct route by road from Ardara to the important monastic sites of Gleann Cholm Cille and Rathlin O'Byrne island. Faced with a journey on foot through solid mist, who could blame the traveller who obeyed the geis and stayed at home?

Gleann na Geise
PASS OF GLENGESH

BRIAN GALLAGHER '00

The caves carved out of the cliff face facing onto the sea at Maghera bring many visitors to this part of the coast. One of the caves was the scene of a gruesome event remembered in the cave's name Uaimh na nDaoine 'the cave of the people'. In this spot hundreds of people were killed in the aftermath of the 1641 Rebellion.

The war and upheaval which characterised the Ireland of the 1640s might seem like just another episode in the troubled history of our island, but it was different in many respects. Although many of the key events took place far away from Donegal - the 'Old English' and Gaelic chieftains met in their own council in Kilkenny and sieges took place throughout the country in Drogheda, Wexford, Cork and Clonmel - Ulster was central to the war. The war was sparked when Gaelic-speaking Catholics in Donegal and throughout Ulster sought to reclaim land given to their new neighbours, many of them Scots, a generation earlier; the leading commander on the Gaelic side was Hugh O'Neill, who led the Ulster Army with distinction; the war more or less ended with the defeat of that field army in Scariffholis, west of Letterkenny in June 1650.

The conflict took place at the same time as the English Civil War, but its causes and the way it evolved were very different. It also differed greatly from the English conflict in the scale of casualties; whereas 4% of the population of England died between 1640 and 1650, the loss of life in Ireland was many times that. It was the ferocity that marked the war in Ulster that casts its pall even today over the natural beauty of the coastline of Maghera.

The tide had turned against the Gaels with the arrival of a 10,000 strong Scots Covenanter force in 1642, and the spread of communal violence forced a group of people from the area to take refuge in Uaimh na nDaoine at Maghera. They were discovered, however, and local lore says that more than five hundred were slaughtered by the Cromwellian side in the cave; only one man survived by concealing himself on a ledge above the awful scenes.

Maghera

BRIAN GALLAGHER 00

Anyone planning to explore Southwest Donegal could hardly do better than bring with them a copy of *In Conall's Footsteps* by Lochlann McGill; provided, that is, they already own a pair of sturdy walking boots, and are not averse to the great outdoors. By tracing the traditions associated with the sixth century Saint Conall, up mountain and down glen, from Doochary on the Gweebarra River, to Inver, the book gives a unique insight into Southwest Donegal. The heart of the book is the area around Ardara, Lochlann McGill's native place, and the town whose history was so lovingly recorded by his father, P.J. McGill.

Ardara is a town that inspires such love. Nineteenth century visitors to Southwest Donegal tended to be impressed both by the village itself and the countryside they passed through on their way here, and Ardara remains an attractive place: a traditional Donegal town which has held onto its small shops and pubs, when other towns have grown to regret the passing of such institutions of community life. Shops where you can buy woollen goods for example, but also fishing licenses and tackle, as well as getting useful advice on fishing into the bargain.

It is for its woollen goods and tweed that Ardara is best known. Spinning and weaving, while not as old as the hills, have been practised in Southwest Donegal as long as people have lived here, but by the mid nineteenth century the weaving trade was in decline here and all over Ireland.

In the Ardara area a number of people helped to put the trade back on its feet from the 1870s on, including Neil McNelis, who established a hand-spun cottage industry; Mrs. Ernest Hart, who revived the art of dyeing; and the Gillespie Brothers, originally from County Down, who made high quality looms. The revival was enormously boosted when the Congested Districts Board (CDB) was set up in 1891. The CDB established the Market House in 1912, which quickly became the focus of the industry, and a centre for measuring and inspecting the tweed, and a place where the hand crafted produce could be stored and sold. Ardara is now a Heritage Theme Town, one of a small number of such towns in Ireland, with a special focus on its weaving heritage.

BRIAN GALLAGHER 05

On the road from Ardara to Portnoo in the centre of the Dawros peninsula is this portal tomb at Kilclooney, one of the most striking sights in County Donegal. This monument is one of Donegal's emblematic sights, so much so that it was chosen for the front cover of the definitive book on the county's archaeology. There are two portal tombs in Kilclooney, although this one is the better known and more intact of the two. To the passing tourist they may seem an extravagant left over from a forgotten time, but they have much to tell us of the time when Ireland changed from a land of hunter-gatherers to one of farmers.

Between 5,000 and 6,000 years ago the coastal areas of Donegal were inhabited by the people who initiated what we call the Neolithic period. As they began to find it less and less easy to live off the environment - taking food from edible plants and hunting and fishing for wild animals to eat - they turned to modifying their environment - clearing trees and scrub, keeping goats and other animals in herds, and tilling the ground with the beginnings of agricultural implements. How such people came to live in Southwest Donegal or where they came from is not so clear; there is evidence linking Irish settlements of the Neolithic era both to Britain and to continental Europe. What is clear, however, is the importance they placed on giving their dead a proper burial, which is why we have monuments like the Kilclooney portal tombs, just two of the almost 140 Neolithic tombs recorded in County Donegal.

Monuments such as these are often called dolmens, from two Breton words dol and men meaning table and stone respectively. Portal tombs are one of four main types of Neolithic tombs, the others being court tombs, passage tombs (like Newgrange) and wedge tombs. In the Kilclooney portal tombs and others, two large stones in front (each around 1.7m high) with a lower backstone support a huge roofstone, which is 4.3m long. The remains of dead members of the community, possibly the more prosperous or powerful ones, were placed in the burial chambers. The whole tomb was originally covered in a cairn of stones, but most of these were removed over the centuries to build other structures in the area.

From a certain angle the huge roofstone looks like a bird of prey about to swoop. Given the size of the stones here in Kilclooney we can only wonder at how our ancestors brought them here and erected them. Kilclooney remains an awesome place.

Kilclooney

BRIAN GALLAGHER '99

Variously known as 'Doon Fort', 'O'Boyle's Fort' or 'The Bawan', this oval shaped fort is like a Grianán of Aileach set in water. It is a cashel, a ringfort enclosed by a drystone wall, one of well over two hundred in County Donegal, although this and the Grianán are the best known and most evocative. Anyone wishing to see it at close quarters can hire a boat to row across the lough.

Doon Fort takes up almost the entire area of the little island in Loughadoon, so much so that when making your way across the lough you might think that the fort is floating on the water. It has the appearance of a defensive structure, as the walls are almost 3.35 metres above the internal floor, and the floor is higher than the ground outside, giving defenders a clear advantage over attackers, but not everyone agrees that this is why it was built. Archaeologists give four main reasons why a major ancient structure was built: to bury the dead, as a home, for military reasons, and for ritual or ceremonial reasons. The terraced walls of some forts and the parapet which usually runs along the top could also mean that these were small amphitheatres, intended for people looking towards the centre at a ritual event, rather than looking outward at attackers. As there is no terracing at Doon Fort and perhaps more to the point, because of its location there are strong reasons for accepting the local view that it was built for defence.

As with so many ancient structures it is showing signs of decay, with one wall partly collapsed. Doon Fort used to look worse, as sixty years ago the eminent natural historian Robert Lloyd Praeger wrote

"all that is now standing - about half the circumference of the wall - is original work, beautifully dry-built of the local slatey rock, and densely covered with a shaggy coat of grey lichen".

The concerns of Lloyd Praeger and other seems to have prompted the authorities to act as in the mid 1950s the fort was 'restored' to its present state. It was apparently used by poitín makers in an earlier era, and their illicit huts were removed from the fort at that same time.

Doon Fort

Brian Friel, whose mother came from nearby Glenties, gives his characters this exchange in his play *Living Quarters*. Portnoo is a small but attractive holiday resort on the northern shore of the Dawros peninsula, a sister village to Narin barely a mile along the coast. Both of them are very popular with visitors from Northern Ireland.

This is as good a place as any to take the sea air, with the Atlantic rolling in towards the sandy beach which stretches to the east past Narin. Although Portnoo faces north into the Atlantic, the hills to the west on Dunmore Head offer very welcome protection. The rocks on the shore near the pier tell the story of how this part of Donegal was formed, millions of years ago: you can see slates run through with veins of granite, and black crystalline limestone showing the effects of millennia of erosion by rain and sea spray.

Looking out to sea the first sight is the island of Inishkeel, Inis Caoil in Gaelic, which gives its name to the local parish, including the town of Glenties. Beyond Inishkeel one can see the estuary of the Gweebarra River and the southern edge of the Rosses. When the tide is low one can walk from Narin out to the island which is named after Conall Caol, the sixth century saint who is associated with many other places in the southwest of the county. The tide allows you around an hour to visit the sites, before walking back again. It is well worth a visit, with its early Christian churches, holy wells and beautifully decorated stone slabs. Inishkeel used to attract many locals to do the 'stations', the traditional ritual of walking around sites connected to a saint and saying prayers in his honour. We have seen a similar ritual or turas in Gleann Cholm Cille.

Erosion has made the island more distant from the mainland; only a couple of generations ago Inishkeel was apparently near enough for people to throw a stone across from the mainland.

Portnoo

BRIAN GALLAGHER '99

The little town of Glenties, located where a number of glens meet, is proud of its reputation as an attractive place, and of its literary connections. It is a five-time winner of the title of Ireland's Tidiest Town; in 1958, 1959, 1960, 1962 and most recently in 1995. This success is, no doubt, helped by its splendid location, but is primarily down to the great community spirit of the townspeople.

A little over a century ago the area's most famous son was born, a man who would go on to become an acclaimed writer despite his very modest beginnings. In due course he would lend his name to a cultural festival which has brought renown and no little money to his native town.

Patrick MacGill, 'the Navvy Poet' was born on New Year's Day 1891, the eldest of eleven children. Like so many before and after him in the west of the county, he was sent to the Hiring Fair in Strabane at the age of twelve, to be hired out to a farmer on the more fertile land of Mid-Ulster. He soon moved to Scotland, again like so many of his countymen, working first as a tatie-hoker in Ayrshire, picking potatoes on the farms, and not long after opting for the life of a navvy.

What was to mark MacGill apart, however, and make his name remembered, was his single-mindedness in making up for his lack of formal education back in Glenties, devoting himself to reading and learning. He was still a young man when he began to write; his first book of poems, entitled *Gleanings from a Navvy's Scrapbook*, was published in 1911, when he was barely 20.

MacGill never forgot the conditions which first prompted him to leave Glenties: the locally powerful well-connected traders whose greed and vindictiveness kept small farmers and labourers in hock inspired much of his writing, most notably *Children of the Dead End: the autobiography of a Navvy*, published in 1914. This important thread in his early writings did not endear him to everyone back in Glenties, where some of his thinly disguised characters and their relatives were still prominent in the life of the town. MacGill's standing locally is now secure, and he is honoured each August when the MacGill Summer School brings scholars and commentators to the Highlands Hotel for a week of lectures, exhibitions, and night-time entertainment.

Glenties

BRIAN GALLAGHER 00

The range of rounded hills north of Donegal Bay known as the Croaghs, or Blue Stacks or in Irish na Cruacha Gorma, could be said to be at the heart of Donegal. Driving north towards Donegal Town they are a distinct purple blue presence on the horizon, as they are if you are travelling towards Fintown from Letterkenny on the way to the west or southwest of the county. It was to this spot that an American couple came in 1970 to get away from the rat race.

It is not unusual for people to leave the cities and set up home in remote parts of Ireland, and to subsequently write about the life and traditions of the area - this strand is at least as old as J. M. Synge. But few writers have captured a different way of life as beautifully as Bob Bernen did in his *Tales from the Blue Stacks* published in 1978 and *The Hills: more tales from the Blue Stacks* published 5 years later. Bob Bernen had begun teaching Classics at Harvard when still in his twenties, and could have had a prestigious life in academia, had he not been drawn to this remote part of northwest Ireland. Bernen's stories show how the qualities which attracted him to the Classics could be found in living men and women in the Croaghs "the Greek awe of nature and its wonders, the Roman fascination with men and their ordinary lives, the Hebrew commitment to life".

Experiencing this place which so engrossed Bernen is a little easier today, now that community groups in the Croaghs and neighbouring parts of South Donegal have prepared a marked walking route through the area, called Slí na gCruacha Gorma. The Slí, measuring around 75 miles or 120 km allows walkers to travel from Ardara through the Croaghs to Pettigo where it connects with the Ulster Way. The Slí will also allow walkers to branch off at Comeen onto another route through the Donegal Gaeltacht, known as Bealach na Gaeltachta. Walkers will be able to appreciate at first hand the natural beauty of the area, and stay at guesthouses along the way.

Na Cruacha Gorma
THE BLUE STACKS

BRIAN GALLACHER '00

The 'Big Gap' - Bearnas Mór - was created by a glacier which scooped all before it. Barnesmore is both the link and the dividing point between North and South Donegal, so it is no surprise to learn that the Gap was probably fashioned by a glacial movement seeking an outlet to the south. This view of how the Gap was created is borne out by the eskers - the ridges of sand and gravel - which are so common in the Gap, and which have provided building materials for generations of local people.

Through Barnesmore ran the great bealach or highway of Tír Chonaill, joining Donegal Town with an important ford on the river Finn; on one side of this ford was Srath Bó Féich (the 'flat ground near a river where Foy's cows grazed', from which Ballybofey takes its name) and on the other Srath an Urláir, modern day Stranorlar. The Gap did not only divide north and south, however. The prominent hill to the east of the Gap, near Lough Mourne, is Croaghonagh, or Cruach Eoghanach, signifying the western boundary of Cenel or Tír Eoghain, while the hill facing it on the western side is Croaghconnelagh or Cruach Conallach, the frontier of Tír Chonaill.

Local tradition used to maintain that the Gap was home to groups of thieves and outlaws, the "ancient woodkerne of Ireland". Baron Finglas, the Chief Baron of Ireland in 1529, noted that Barnesmore was the most dangerous and least traversable of all of the passes in Ireland, and recommended to the Lord Deputy that an armed force should spend part of each Summer cutting a path through the woods at the approaches to the Gap. Later that century, when Don Alonzo Cobo, a Spanish envoy, was making his way from Killybegs to meet the O'Donnell chieftain in Lifford, he had to be accompanied by an armed group of Sweeneys and Boyles to guarantee his safety. Lughaidh Ó Cléirigh, the biographer of Aodh Ruadh II Ó Domhnaill, credited his hero with solving the problem

"this Barnesmore is an intricate mountain to pass over and it was a refuge for robbers and rogues, robbing and plundering, until Hugh Roe banished them".

With the Donegal Town by-pass, and the greatly improved road from Clar to the edge of Barnesmore, nearing completion at the time of writing, those days of difficult and dangerous travel seem very far away indeed.

Barnesmore

BRIAN GALLAGHER '00.

The area around this lake is as renowned for its history as its beauty. The Lough feeds the River Eske, the river that flows through Donegal Town to the sea, passing Donegal Castle on the way.

At the northern end of the Lough, under the shadow of the Croaghs or Blue Stack Mountains, is Inishgarve, also known as Moylederg Island. Excavations during the 1940s exposed evidence of human habitation ranging from Neolithic to medieval times. In the closing decades of the sixteenth and early decades of the seventeenth centuries, one of the main O'Donnell castles was on O'Donnell's Island, near the southern shore. This was Niall Garbh Ó Domhnaill's main residence. The remains of the castle and bawn are still to be seen, although they are not easy to find due to the vegetation which has covered the island for many years.

When the Brooke family took possession of the O'Donnell lands at the time of the Ulster Plantation, they gained the Lough and the area around it. Soon after beginning the work of extending and enhancing Donegal Castle, they began building a residence on the south western shore of the Lough. It was only in the nineteenth century, however, that the building took on the grand appearance for which Lough Eske Castle came to be known. The Brooke connection lasted until 1894, when Colonel de Vere Brooke sold Lough Eske Castle to Major General Henry White.

Between then and the 1980s the estate passed through the hands of a succession of owners: Henry Knee - who ran it as a guest house; Scott Swan; and an American named Bernard Etzin; before finally being bought by Coillte, the state owned forestry development agency. The Castle had been partially destroyed in 1939, and had deteriorated in the decades after. It is now a ruin.

Lough Eske Castle is not the only fine residence on the Lough Shore. On the eastern side is Ardnamona, a shooting lodge begun sometime around 1790 by Sir Thomas Brooke. Ardnamona was also eventually bought by Coillte, but is now in private hands. The gardens are being restored, and the house now welcomes paying guests.

Lough Eske

In medieval times no kingdom or principality could be without its own holy place: France had Tours, Germany had Aachen and England had Canterbury. The Irish equivalent was not the ecclesiastical capital of Armagh, nor any of the relatively prosperous cities of the east or south, but St. Patrick's Purgatory on an island in Lough Derg where counties Donegal and Fermanagh meet. Indeed in 1492, the year that Christopher Columbus sailed the ocean blue to discover America, a map of the known world was produced showing only one place marked in Ireland - Lough Derg.

Medieval pilgrimages to Lough Derg, Santiago de Compostela and other sites played a key role in building a common Christian experience in Europe, and we have accounts written by pilgrims from France, Hungary, the Netherlands, and Spain as well as Ireland and England telling of their travels to and from this rather bleak place. The Reformation changed all that of course, making Ireland inaccessible to continental pilgrims, but Lough Derg has never lost its pull on Irish people.

The established church took a poor view of the continuation of pilgrimages. When this area was surveyed by Lt. Lancey of the Royal Engineers in 1835 he was much amused by the fact that

"the ferry is kept by a Protestant (who) rents from the executive of the late Colonel Leslie at 65 pounds a year".

Lancey also advised that

"the best way to see this place to advantage is to row round it, as the prior stops everything directly a Protestant lands on its shores."

This advice was redundant for believers, however. Right up to the present day droves of people come each year to Pettigo and cross on the ferries to atone for sins and pray for deliverance from ills that afflict them or their loved ones, although the penance is by all accounts less harsh than it used to be. Until the Great Northern Railway closed in the late 1950s, the train brought many people here from distant parts of the country, a journey now made by bus and car. All over Ireland on church bulletin boards and in shop windows one can still see notices advertising parish or diocesan pilgrimages to Lough Derg. St. Patrick's Purgatory is still drawing its pilgrims.

Lough Derg

BRIAN GALLAGHER OO.

Bundoran is an unashamedly good-time seaside resort, where more than the sea air is bracing - 'Bundoran: the playground of Ireland' or 'The Brighton of Ireland' as the local publicity has it. The hoteliers and the owners of guesthouses and places of entertainment reckon that "there is no limit to the variety of attractions" here, and that the "holiday spirit is always so much in evidence". It is interesting to note that at one time it looked like Bundoran would not develop as a holiday resort; indeed Bundoran itself did not exist as a place up until comparatively recently.

The area between the River Drowse, which today marks the boundary with Sligo, the River Erne and the ocean has always been recognised as a distinct geographical and ecclesiastical entity. It was known as Magh Ene, which is still the official name of the parish which gives the Diocese of Clogher access to the sea. The name Bundoran (from bun dobhráin, meaning the place where a little stream of water enters the sea, i.e. the inlet near the Allingham Hotel) was first noted in 1777. The first inkling that it might develop as a holiday resort was when Viscount Enniskillen built 'Bundoran Lodge' early in the nineteenth century as a summer house, similar to those which had become very popular on the south coast of England. At that time there were two separate villages - Bundoran which referred to what is today called the West End, and Single Street, about a mile away towards Ballyshannon. Well into the second half of the nineteenth century the two villages were separate, with the original

Bundoran remaining a small and genteel watering hole for the better off. When a plan was mooted to attract a wider public from the growing industrial workforce of east Ulster, a local landowner attempted to block the right of way to the sea. This dispute ended up in the High Court in Dublin with the judge finding for the plaintiffs who wanted to secure the right of way. This was a turning point in the development of Bundoran. By the early twentieth century the town had grown into the vastly popular resort that was envisaged back then, and has retained its popularity; interestingly on a walk along the seafront you can still see the different character of the buildings at the West End.

Bundoran

BRIAN GALLAGHER .00

Ballyshannon has something of the border town about it. Although the county boundary is four miles further on at the Drowes River, the Erne which flows through Ballyshannon marked the southern boundary of historical Tír Chonaill, and still divides the dioceses of Raphoe and Clogher. There is something different about the Ballyshannon accent; it has more in common with West Fermanagh and North Leitrim, despite the fact that Donegal Town is only some fourteen miles to the north, a short journey by the fine road that was opened in the early 1980s.

Ballyshannon had long been an important stronghold for the O'Donnells. Although the Erne was, as we have seen, a historical frontier, for long periods the reach of the O'Donnells extended much further, beyond the river Drowes and into North Sligo, and eastwards into Maguire country. It was because of a perceived vulnerability to attack from Connacht that Niall Garbh O Domhnaill built the castle in Ballyshannon in 1423. This remained one of the chief seats of O'Donnell power, until the O'Donnells themselves had to give way to a stronger force. It was from Ballyshannon Castle that Aodh Ruadh II set out in 1592 for his inauguration at the traditional centre of Doon Rock in the north of the county.

Important though the castle was in its time, Ballyshannon is in essence an eighteenth and nineteenth century town. A well known early nineteenth century

print shows the town climbing the hill, above the bridge. Along the Mall you can see some of the fine eighteenth century houses, including the Condon House which has, admittedly, seen better days. Ballyshannon received its first patent to hold a weekly market in August of 1639, but it had been an important centre of trade and learning for many centuries before that. Because of its crucial position on the Erne it has always been a gateway to Donegal and the west of Ulster. Ballyshannon was a trading port, and a prosperous one supplying not only South Donegal but Fermanagh and Cavan, until ships grew so big that they found the bar at the mouth of the Erne too great an obstacle.

Ballyshannon

BRIAN GALLAGHER '99

The Erne gives the town of Ballyshannon much of its character. One of the earliest stories relating to the area tells of how the Assaroe waterfall got its name. Some two thousand years ago the kingship of Ireland was given to three princes, the sons of three brothers, to hold for seven years each in rotation. One of them was named Aodh Ruadh, a name that was to prove very popular in the history of Donegal. Towards the end of his third period of kingship, when he was an old man, he fell into the river and drowned. He was buried on the hill overlooking the waterfall, and from then on it was known as Eas (Aoidh) Ruadh (the waterfall of Red Hugh).

The river provided the town's best known poet, William Allingham, with the inspiration for some of his best known poems. Allingham was born in Ballyshannon in 1824, two days after St. Patrick's Day. His first job was in a bank in the town, but he joined the civil service at the age of twenty two, and was posted as a Customs official on the south coast of Donegal. In 1863 he was transferred to Lymington in Hampshire and remained in the job until 1870. His first book was published in 1858, and he continued to write and be published until his death in 1889. Despite moving in literary circles and receiving praise from fellow writers such as Ruskin, Turgenev and Tennyson, Allingham never loosened his emotional ties to Ballyshannon, as these lines show:

"The music of the waterfall, the mirror of the tide,

When all the green-hill'd harbour is full from side to side -
From Portnasun to Bulliebawns, and round the Abbey Bay,
From rocky Inis Saimer to Coolnargit sandhills grey;
While far upon the southern line, to guard it like a wall,
The Leitrim mountains clothed in blue gaze calmly over all,
And watch the ship sail up or down, the red flag at her stern:
Adieu to these, adieu to all the winding banks of Erne".

Ballyshannon
'THE WINDING BANKS OF ERNE'

BRIAN GALLAGHER '00

The sight of members of the Orange Order making their way through the narrow country roads in Rossnowlagh is no longer news. The annual celebration of the Twelfth of July in this seaside village has become a fixture on the calendar. The parade actually takes place not on the Twelfth itself, but on the preceding Saturday, the change of day enabling Orange brethren and marching bands to come from Northern Ireland and from Cavan and Monaghan.

The Rossnowlagh parade has for many years been the only Twelfth celebration in the Republic, but earlier in the twentieth century parades used to be held at nearby Ballintra and Brownhall, and in the Lagan. There are a number of Lodges in the south of the county, from Bruckless to Ballintra, and holding the parade in a popular holiday resort makes the day out all the more attractive.

The Twelfth of July march is not the only reason to visit Rossnowlagh. Belalt strand, more commonly known as Rossnowlagh strand, is one of the finest in Ireland, and in recent years has become very popular with surfers not only from this country but from all over Europe and further afield. It faces west towards the Atlantic, an expanse of not quite golden sand stretching some 3 km / almost 2 miles from north to south. It is of course the waves from the Atlantic which attract the visitors, rather than the sand, or let's be honest the sun. There are hills at either end of the strand, which allow you to have a good view of the sport when the surfers are out. Belalt strand has suffered greatly from erosion, and it is possible to see graphic evidence of this. Embedded in the sand are the remains of a pillbox originally erected on the bank overlooking the strand in the 1940s, but which subsequently fell when the bank was eroded. This is now more than 25 metres from the shoreline, thus in a little over half a century the sea has taken some 30 metres from the land.

Just south of the strand in the townland of Coolmore stands a Franciscan Friary. The Franciscans have had links with South Donegal since the founding of the Friary outside Donegal Town in the 1470s. *The Annals of the Four Masters* were written by four Franciscan friars at nearby Bundrowes, and it was the tercentenary of the death of the leader of the Four Masters, Micheál Ó Cleirigh, in 1944 which prompted the return of the Francsicans to the area. In 1946 the Friars took over Belalt House, formerly owned by the trustees of the Shiel Hospital in Ballyshannon. A new Friary was built in 1952, and this is home to a small community who are proud of re-establishing the links between Donegal and the Franciscans.

Rossnowlagh

BRIAN GALLAGHER '99

The parish of Drumholm, with its two small towns of Ballintra, pictured here, and Laghey, is a quiet area between Donegal Town and Ballyshannon. These are not only the main towns of South Donegal, but the two most historic towns in the county, yet Drumholm has its own story to tell.

Drumholm is very proud of its associations with Adhamhnán, also known as Adomnan or, in English, Eunan. Adhamhnán is the patron of the Diocese of Raphoe, and the most famous and interesting successor to Colm Cille as Abbot of Iona. While tradition holds Adhamhnán (born ca. 624) was from Drumholm, modern scholars believe this may not necessarily be the case; he certainly received his education there, but it was usual for young men to move away from home to study for the church.

Whether or not Adhamhnán was a native of Drumholm or merely spent his formative years here, he certainly 'came from decent people', as the song says about St. Patrick. His family tree shows that he came from a distinguished line of the Cenel Chonaill, one which had produced three High Kings of Ireland. His mother's name was Rónnat and his father's was Rónán. Adhamhnán, while no doubt conscious of his lineage, never seems to have made much of it, instead deciding to devote himself to a life in the church.

Although patron of the diocese of Raphoe, it is not clear whether he was Abbot of the monastery in Raphoe which gave its name to the diocese. We know that he moved to Colm Cille's foundation on the island of Iona, and was elected Abbot in 679 and remained in that position for a quarter of a century, until 704. One of his achievements there was to write *Vita Sancti Columbae*, the first biography of his kinsman Colm Cille described as 'the most considerable surviving literary production of the Celtic church in Ireland'.

Ballintra

BRIAN GALLAGHER '00

South of Donegal Town, and before the junction with the recently completed by-pass, is a signpost for St. Ernan's. Many drivers pass by every day without giving it a second glance, but it is worth a little detour.

Up until the passing of the Land Acts this area was the property of the Hamilton family, landlords who were respected by their tenants, no mean feat in a county known for landlords such as John George Adair and the Earl of Leitrim. Though their modest estate was in a comparatively remote part of the country, they were well connected with the Anglo-Irish nobility; the most famous of the Hamiltons, John, who died in 1884, could claim people like the Earl of Longford and even the Duke of Wellington as uncles. The Hamiltons came to Donegal in the seventeenth century from Scotland, where one Gilbert of Hamildone had founded the line. They were well connected there as well; the first Lord Hamilton was a son of the daughter of King James II – not to be confused with James II of England, who was James VII of Scotland – and his own son James became the first Earl of Arran.

Although they had first lived in Murvagh, the principal Brownhall residence was around 1 mile east of the village of Ballintra. This was originally built as a two storey house in the late seventeenth or early eighteenth century, and a much larger three storey structure was added in 1794. This house was built on leasehold land, however - leased from Trinity College in Dublin - and when John Hamilton inherited the estate on his twenty first birthday in 1821, he soon resolved to build a house on his own freehold land. In 1824 he began work on the 'cottage' on St. Ernan's island in Donegal Bay - the building which is now a small hotel.

It quickly became obvious that having a home on an island had its disadvantages, so he set about building a causeway. This was no easy task given the strong tides in the area, and it looked at times as if he might be beaten by the forces of nature. He had not counted on his tenants, however. Hamilton's diary records his surprise when bands of them, both Protestant ("all Orangemen, fine stout fellows, but hot-blooded") and Catholic ("most of them ... Ribbonmen"), offered their services free of charge. The causeway was soon built, and is still there today. A stone plaque, on the causeway shown in the painting was fixed to the wall after Hamilton's death in 1884; the inscription on it begins,

This causeway stands to commemorate the great mutual love between John Hamilton and the people of Donegal, both his tenants and others, through a time of bitter famine and pestilence ...

St. Ernan's, Donegal Town

BRIAN GALLAGHER '90

HOTEL

The People of South Donegal

Tír Chonaill, Tirconnell, County Donegal - these are the names which have been used over the centuries to describe Ireland's northernmost county. Although 'County Donegal' is the name now generally used, Gaelic speakers in the west and southwest of the County still call their native place 'Tír Chonaill'. Like its neighbouring county, Tyrone (or Tír Eoghain), the name Tír Chonaill reminds us that this is a territory associated with a powerful historical figure. Conal and Eoghan lived well over a thousand years ago - and don't ever suggest to a Donegal man that they are only legendary figures! - but their memory lives on, having together given their names to the greater part of west Ulster. They were brothers, sons of the equally famous Niall Noigiallach or Niall of the Nine Hostages.

While the stories that have come down to us about Niall Noigiallach should not be treated as historical fact, they contain at least a nugget of truth. The ancient Irish annals tell us that Niall lived in the latter half of the fourth century, ruling as Árd Rí or High King of Ireland from 379-405. He was married twice, and with each of his wives founded powerful and long-lasting dynasties; his sons by his first wife were the first of the Southern Uí Néill, based in what is now County Meath, while his sons by his second wife - these included Conall, Eoghan and Éanna - founded the Northern Uí Néill. Much of the Ulster Cycle, one of the four great collections of tales in early Gaelic literature, tells of the attempts of the previous rulers of the northern part of Ireland to resist the rise of the Northern Uí Néill. These attempts were of little avail in the end, but gave us the great stories of Cú Chulainn, The Táin and so on.

The history of the 1200 years - from the fourth to the sixteenth centuries - of the western part of Ulster, and especially of Donegal, is by and large the story of Niall's descendants. Amongst the descendants of his son Conall, for instance, were 41 saints and 10 High Kings, perhaps the most famous of them being Colm Cille, a man who could have been High King, but opted instead for a life in the church; Colm Cille was arguably the greatest figure the county ever produced, and is remembered in many parts of the south of the county, most notably in the valley to which he gave his name - Gleann Cholm Cille or Glencolumbkille.

Conall was an important figure not only because he has given his name to this county. His full name was Conall Gulban, some sources say from 'Ben Gulban' an earlier form of Ben Bulben, the mountain which dominates the most southerly part of Donegal and neighbouring Sligo. Conall Gulban is not to be confused with another Conall, the sixth century saint who is intimately linked with southwest Donegal, and whom we shall be meeting later.

The people linked by blood and loyalty to the powerful Gaelic figures in history were collectively known as 'Cenel', which broadly means 'kindred of' or 'people of'. Thus the Cenel Chonaill were the kindred/people of Conall. The territory in which they lived was known as Tír Chonaill, the 'land of Conall' or, perhaps more appropriately, the 'land of the people of Conall'. As we have seen the people associated with Conall's brother Eoghan were known as the Cenel Eoghain, and they occupied Tír Eoghain, later anglicised as Tyrone.

Tír Chonaill has been recognised as a distinct place - or to be exact, a grouping of distinct places - for many centuries. South and southwest Tír Chonaill, the area covered by this book, comprised the district of Tír Aodha and most of the neighbouring district of Tír Baghaine. Tír Aodha (the land of Aodh or Hugh, modern Tirhugh) stretches from the Eany Water near Inver to Assaroe on the River Erne. The Aodh after whom the area was called was the Aodh Ruadh who also gave his name to the Assaroe falls - Eas Ruaidh the waterfall of (Aodh) Ruadh; thus Tirhugh is the only one of the major divisions of Tír Chonaill not called after a descendant of Niall Noigiallach. Tír Baghaine (modern Banagh, which takes its name from Éanna Baghainne, one of the seven sons of Conall), includes all the territory west of the Eany Water and south of the river Dobhar, which marks the southern boundary of Gaoth Dobhair (Gweedore). The remainder of 'Conall's territory' comprised Tír Luighdheach and Tír Éanna in the north and east of the county. Magh Éine, between the rivers Erne and Drowes, did not form part of historical Tír Chonaill, but became officially part of County Donegal when the County was shired in 1585.

These territorial names were first written down some 1,000 years ago, a little before surnames began to be used in Ireland. In choosing a surname families looked to an ancestor held in high regard; if that ancestor was their father the surname took a 'Mac' form, eg. Mac Rabhartaigh (Magroarty) or Mac Giolla Bhrighde (McBride). If they wished to be associated with their grandfather or someone from a previous generation the surname took an 'Ua' or 'Ó' form, from ua, meaning grandson. The surname O'Donnell, the best known Donegal family name, entered history towards the end of the eleventh century when the family decided to take their name from their great grandfather Domhnall, son of Éicnechán, who was King of Cenel Conaill until his death in 906. Éicnechán's own father was named Dálach, and the name Clann Dálaigh or Síl Dálaigh which is often used to describe the O'Donnells, derives from him.

Important as they were, the story of Donegal did not begin with the Cenel

Chonaill. There may be no recorded history for the pre-Christian period, but there is a wealth of folklore and mythology. The *Annála Rioghachta Éirinn*, better known as the *Annals of the Four Masters*, were compiled by four friars at the Franciscan house at Bundrowes, outside Bundoran, between 1632 and 1636. They used older manuscript sources and the oral tradition to create what was until modern times the most important single account of Irish history. When it came to selecting what went into the *Annals of the Four Masters*, there was no shortage of traditions and lore to choose from, a considerable amount of it relating to South Donegal.

One story tells of how the waterfall on the Erne at Ballyshannon got its name. More than two thousand years ago, some five hundred years before the coming of Christianity, the kingship of Ireland was given to three men for each of them to hold it in rotation for a period of seven years. The three were cousins, sons of three brothers: Aodh Ruadh, son of Badurn, Dithorba, son of Deman, and Kimbath, son of Fintan. Aodh Ruadh was given the honour of holding the kingship for the first seven-year period, and held it not once but three times. Towards the end of his third period, which must have been some fifty years after his first term, he was crossing the River Erne at a ford and fell in. His body was washed down over the waterfall, and when recovered, was buried on the hill overlooking the scene of the tragedy. Ever after the waterfall has been called Eas Ruaidh (the cataract of (Aodh) Ruadh) or Assaroe. The story did not end there, however. Aodh Ruadh's only child was Macha, known as 'Macha of the Golden Hair', who claimed the right to succeed her father for the remainder of his term. When the others refused to accept that a woman should accede to the kingship, Macha raised an army and defeated her kinsmen's forces. She agreed to spare their lives on condition that they became her vassals, and enlisted their help in building a large royal enclosure called Eamhan Mhacha in her honour. The remains of this site can still be seen near modern day Armagh, which itself means 'the height of Macha'. It is only fair to point out that macha also means 'a milking place', but then why ruin a good story?

Five centuries after Aodh Ruadh and Macha, Christianity came to the northern part of Ireland, in the person of Patrick. Tradition records that Patrick himself came to the Erne, blessing the south bank but leaving the northern side to a holy man, i.e. Colm Cille, whose coming he foretold. This story should be read in the context of the times when it evolved. The south bank of the Erne is in Clogher diocese, whereas the other side of the river is in Colm Cille's native Raphoe diocese. Ecclesiastical chroniclers had their eyes on the niceties of their own times when recording events; political correctness is not as recent a phenomenon as one might think. A similar story has come down to us about Patrick's trip to Gleann Cholm Cille.

Some centuries before Patrick, Fionn

Mac Cumhaill was hunting in the area with his favourite hound Bran. When Bran balked at crossing the river Senghleann after a stag, Fionn surmised that 'Colm Cille after whom the valley would be named would come here and also bless many places in Erin and Albain'. Beat that for foresight! Patrick duly came to southwest Donegal, and in converting the natives, drove a pack of demons before him. When they were driven as far as they could go in the glen, they caused a huge fog to descend over the entire area, turning the river Senghleann into a stream of fire. Patrick had to make a strategic withdrawal, but forecast, in an echo of what he said on the banks of the Erne, that one would come and drive the demons out, once and for all.

Cometh the hour, cometh the man. One hundred years on, Colm Cille, who was born near Lough Gartan in the north of the county, approached the glen with his followers. The demons did not take this lightly and killed one of the saint's followers -

Cearc - thus giving rise to the placename Srath na Circe. Colm Cille was not a man to take this lying down so he chased the demons into the sea at a place called Screig na nDeamhan 'the demons' rocky shore'. Having seen off the demons, Colm Cille lost no time in establishing the new religion in the glen. The remains of his foundations can still be seen: Séipéal Cholm Cille near Glen Head, Cill Fhánaid behind the holiday village, Teampall Chaoimhín in Malinbeg, and Teampall na Manach near the Murlin River. Colm Cille is remembered above all, each June 9th, the anniversary of his death, when locals and pilgrims complete the turas or devotional journey, in his honour.

Gleann Cholm Cille is the only one of Colm Cille's many foundations in Donegal which bears his name. This is something of which the people of the parish are rightly proud, but there are many other places in South Donegal which treasure their early Christian heritage. There are three other figures who loom large in the ecclesiastical

history of the area: Finnian, Adhamhnán, and Conall.

Given the pre-eminence of Colm Cille in Irish Christianity, and especially in Donegal, it is remarkable that all the sources acknowledge the saint's debt to another figure, his teacher and to some extent, role model, a saint called Finnian. Whereas we know quite a lot about Colm Cille - his date and place of birth, his parentage, his career, and date of death - Finnian is, like St Patrick, a shadowy figure in comparison. We might note in passing that it would be more historically accurate to say 'St. Patricks', as the figure whom Ireland honours as its national saint is a composite of three or more historical persons. Recent research, especially by Prof. Pádraig Ó Riain, has helped to clear up much of the uncertainty about Finnian. For many years there was confusion about whether Colm Cille's teacher was Finnian of Movilla (in County Down) or Finnian of Clonard (in County Meath). Prof. Ó Riain provides strong evidence that these

Finnians were one and the same, and that he was born in Britain, most probably in Wales, the son of Irish parents. Confusion was understandable, however, given that the elder saint was known under a variety of names - Finnian, Finnio, Barrfhionn, and Fionnbarr. It is under one of these names - Barrfhionn - that he is honoured in Ballyshannon, where the name of the parish, Kilbarron (Cill Barrfhionn) means the church of fair-haired Fionn / Finnian. Kilbarron's nearest neighbour to the north is the parish of Drumholm, where the church was founded by Colm Cille, and where Adhamhnán received his education. The juxtaposition of saints was a frequent refrain in early Irish hagiography, and says much about the importance of this part of South Donegal in Columban and early medieval times. Finnian is honoured in many other ecclesiastical foundations throughout Ireland, most notably as Fionnbarr of Cork.

Colm Cille's most famous successor as Abbot of Iona was his kinsman, Adhamhnán, or Adomnán, or Eunan. Adhamhnán was born to Rónnat and her husband Rónán sometime around 624, a little over a quarter of a century after Colm Cille's death. He came from a distinguished line of the Cenel Chonaill, one that had produced three High Kings of Ireland. Adhamhnán in his own writings never made much of his lineage, and seems to have set himself on a life in the church from his youth. Although tradition holds that he was born near Drumholm, the parish between Donegal Town and Ballyshannon, this may not necessarily be the case. He was a postulant there, but we know from other sources that young men often moved away from their home to study for the church.

Following his period of study in Drumholm, Adhamhnán may have been Abbott of Raphoe - he is patron of the diocese of Raphoe - before moving to Iona when Fáilbe was Abbot there. He was elected Abbott in succession to Fáilbe in 679 and remained in that position for a quarter of a century, until 704. During that time he wrote *Vita Sancti Columbae*, the first biography of Colm Cille, completing it around 700 AD. This work has been called 'the most considerable surviving literary production of the Celtic church in Ireland'. While not a biography in the modern sense of the word, it is a remarkable work of early medieval scholarship, an outstanding achievement at a high point of Irish Christianity which saw "a virtual explosion of documentation", as the historian Charles Doherty calls it.

Adhamhnán's writings were concerned not only with the church; he was a legal scholar and lawgiver of the Brehon laws which governed social and economic relations in Ireland until the sixteenth and seventeenth centuries. The Cathedral of Raphoe in Letterkenny, whose centenary will be celebrated in 2001, is fittingly called after these two great monks of the Cenel Chonaill, Colm Cille and Adhamhnán.

While Colm Cille has associations

with Gleann Cholm Cille and Drumholm, and Finnian / Barrfhionn and Adhamhnán are linked with the area between Ballyshannon and Donegal Town, there is one other saint who could be said to be pre-eminent in the area from Mountcharles to Glenties - Conall Caol. Unlike Colm Cille and Adhamhnán, however, we have only fleeting documentary evidence for his life. A number of writers have written about Conal, including Michéal Ó Cléirigh of the Four Masters and John Colgan, both Franciscan annalists, accepting as fact the stories which were handed down in local tradition, and assigning him a family tree that would connect him to Colm Cille. Lochlann MacGill, a well known historian of the area has put forward the view that the Conal honoured in southwest Donegal, is in reality a cleric called Cóelán, who was prominent in East Down in the 5th century. There is no doubting the strength of the local traditions, however, which connect him to many places in Southwest Donegal - such as Loughros Point, Portnoo, Glenties,

Bruckless and above all the island of Inis Caol or Inishkeel.

In the popular mind the history of Donegal is to a great extent the history of the O'Donnells. Although the inauguration site of the O'Donnells was at Doon Rock, near Kilmacrennan in the north of the county, their main castles and residences were at Donegal and Ballyshannon. Given its location at the head of the huge bay where the River Eske enters the sea it is no surprise that Donegal Town should have had a pivotal role in the history of the county and of the O'Donnells. Whether one is going west to Killybegs and Gleann Cholm Cille, or going east and south from there; whether one is going from Connacht to North Donegal and the West of Ulster; or going from Letterkenny or Derry to the west or southwest of Ireland, one has to pass through Donegal Town. While Donegal, i.e. Dún na nGall, has been known by that name for centuries, the place seems to have been previously called Teach na nGall and Áth na nGall, i.e. the 'house of the

foreigners' and 'ford of the foreigners'. When the officials in Dublin Castle came to mark out the boundaries of the county and to decide the location of the county town there was no doubt in their minds that

"the towne of Donnygall is the only place for her majestie's gaole and sheere towne, for her highnes' cessions and jaile deliverie, within the said countye of Donnygall"

No doubt the presence there of the O'Donnell castle was a major consideration. Donegal castle was built by Aodh Ruadh II Ó Domhnaill at the beginning of the sixteenth century on the banks of the Eske. The remains of his tower house and the manor house built by Sir Basil Brooke at right angles to it can still be seen, having been carefully preserved by Dúchas-the Heritage Service in recent years. The ruins of another, earlier, O'Donnell fortress are not far away on O'Donnell's Island in Lough Eske.

Three quarters of a century before

Aodh Ruadh II built Donegal Castle, his predecessor as chieftain, Niall Garbh, built a castle at Ballyshannon. The River Erne marked the traditional boundary with Connacht, although at the height of their power, the O'Donnells' rule extended well beyond the Erne. Niall Garbh's purpose in building the castle was to protect his southern flank against the men of the west. Almost nothing remains of the building, the site of which adjoins the market yard.

The O'Donnells can, with considerable justification, claim pre-eminence in the history of Donegal. It was this family who provided leading figures such as Maghnus O'Donnell, Aodh Dubh and Red Hugh; it was this family which gave rise to the song O'Donnell Abú which evokes Donegal not only to people in the northwest of this island but all over Ireland and throughout the Irish diaspora. It is the O'Donnell arms which form the centrepiece of the county crest. Despite this, however, they controlled Tír Chonaill for only some four centuries,

from the year 1201 to the beginnings of the 1600s. For most of the six centuries before 1201 other families had controlled the kingship between them. In the tenth, eleventh and twelfth centuries the O Canannáin and Ó Mael Doraid families were the leading families of Tír Chonaill.

The first O'Donnell chieftain was Eighneachan, inaugurated in 1200, the first of an unbroken line of twenty five taoisigh or chieftains, the last being Niall Garbh who was inaugurated in 1603 and died in 1625. Although the O'Donnells ruled Tír Chonaill from the beginning of the 13th to the end of the 16th centuries, the Golden Age of Tir Chonaill, if such a phrase can be used, was between the middle of the 15th and the middle of the 16th centuries. Between 1461 and 1555 three chieftains of the O'Donnells - Aodh Rua, Aodh Dubh and Maghnus, father, son and grandson - ruled the territory in succession.These three are recognised as being amongst the great soldier statesmen of Gaelic Ireland. The historian Kenneth Nicholl says

that the O'Donnells "in the fifteenth and sixteenth centuries consistently showed a hardness and a sense of political purpose absent from most Irish rulers". The O'Donnell army succeeded in establishing overlordship of adjoining parts of Fermanagh and North Connacht, as well as over Inishowen and that part of West Tyrone adjoining Donegal. These victories laid the basis for an era still fondly remembered by Donegal people.

This Golden Age was based on three pillars. The political stability which ensued from cohesion within the O'Donnells themselves, their military strength and the support of key allied families were invaluable. Secondly this political stability ushered in an era of comparative prosperity, a prosperity that was all the more remarkable when one considers the fate of the ordinary Gaelic speaking people in other parts of Ireland in that era. Finally, and perhaps most surprisingly, the O'Donnells reaped great benefits from the strong and fruitful links forged with other places beyond Ireland, in Scotland, England and the Continent.

The longstanding loyalty of allied families to the O'Donnell cause - the first pillar - was unique in Gaelic Ireland. Chief amongst these families were the three branches of the Mac Suibhnes, the second best-known Donegal clan or sept - Mac Suibhne Fanad (Sweeney Fanad), Mac Suibhne na dTuath (Sweeney Doe) and Mac Suibhne Baghaineach (Sweeney Banagh). From their original base in the Fanad peninsula in the far north of the county, a branch of the Sweeneys gained possession of territory in Southwest Donegal early in the fourteenth century, taking their name - Mac Suibhne Baghaineach - from the territory they controlled. The main castle of the Mac Suibhne Baghaineach was at Rahan on the St. John's Point peninsula overlooking McSwyne's Bay.

These three branches of the Sweeneys were the backbone of the O'Donnell armies. In addition to these O'Donnell power depended on support from a number of other key families, known as Lucht Tighe or household families. The Uí Baoighill or O'Boyles were very prominent in the Southwest of the county, giving their name to the Barony of Boylagh, as well as O'Boyle's fort on Loughadoon and O'Boyle's Island and castle at Kiltoorish Lake near Rosbeg. Others included the Uí Gallchobhair or Gallaghers, who were the leaders of the O'Donnell cavalry, the Uí Firghil or O'Friels, whose job it was to inaugurate O'Donnell chieftains at Doon Rock, near Kilmacrennan in the north of the county, the Uí Tiomanaigh or Timoneys who specialised in cattle droving, the Uí Cléirigh or O'Clery's who were clerks or scribes to the O'Donnells, and the Mic a'Bháird or Wards, who were the dynastic poets and bards. These family names - Clery, Ward, Timoney, Gallagher, Boyle - are as common as ever in South and Southwest Donegal. The Lucht Tighe were so numerous and so loyal that the O'Donnells could afford to build and hold castles along the marches of their territory with reliable military forces dependent on the O'Donnells themselves. O'Donnell castles were located on the frontier with the O'Neills: in Derry, Lifford, Castlefin, Beleek, and Bundrowes, in addition to the main strongholds in Donegal Town and Ballyshannon. Unlike other great Irish families, for instance the McCarthys in Cork and Kerry, the O'Connors of Connacht, and to a certain extent the neighbouring O'Neills, the O'Donnells did not split up into warring factions amongst themselves, although such factionalism threatened from time to time.

If this period in Donegal's history was a good one for the O'Donnells, their close supporters, and most of the other inhabitants of Tír Chonaill, their neighbours may have had other ideas. The O'Donnells had no hesitation in laying waste to the territory of their rivals. Lughaidh Ó Cléirigh, one of the family of scribes and the biographer of Aodh Ruadh (chieftain 1592-1602) left us an intriguing manuscript account of one such raid (edited and published by the Irish Texts Society in

1948), when the army of Tír Chonaill left South Donegal in the Summer of 1600 and ventured as far south as Clare.

"His troops were gathered together by Ó Domhnaill in the month of June precisely, and they crossed the Saimer, a stream rich in salmon, the Drowes, the Dubh, and the Sligeach, until they came to Ballymote, where the men of Connacht awaited him".

If that seems to describe a fairly benign adventure, the mood changes when they reached County Clare:

"As for Ó Domhnaill, when he had reached Ennis, he sent skirmishers to cover the surrounding country. Far and wide, violently, aggressively, these quick active courageous bodies of men separated from each other, for they traversed and plundered before night."

"There was many a time of plenty for gentlemen, noblemen, and lords of territories with prey and cattle and every sort of spoil".

The account also tells of how his men enjoyed themselves when the battle was won:

"They made neither huts nor buildings, owing to the heat of the summer weather, but they lighted bright, flaming fires, and their attendants and servers, their cooks and houseboys, their ostlers and their soldiers . . . consumed their feast and slept soundly, as they had cast aside their fear".

During this time, when it is not too fanciful to state that Donegal resembled a kind of Gaelic Prussia, the region was anything but economically depressed, its relative prosperity being the second pillar of O'Donnell power. It had a fairly small population concentrated in the fertile parts of Donegal - especially around Donegal Bay. Medieval Tír Chonaill was known for both its cattle and sheep, but also grew large quantities of oats. The fact that the upland areas in the north and west were not heavily populated meant that they could be used for summer pastures, for cutting turf, and as woodlands to provide timber for various purposes, from building houses to building boats. The people used the rivers and the sea fisheries intelligently, and in fact on the continent as well as in Ireland the chieftain of the O'Donnells was known as the

"best lord of fish in Ireland, and he exchangeth fish always with foreign merchants for wine, by which [he] is called in other countries, the king of fish".

The ports of Ballyshannon, Donegal and Killybegs were crucial to this trade. Even before the beginning of this era Tír Chonaill had established trading links with ports outside Ireland, the third pillar on which the Golden Age rested. They had flourishing links with a number of ports in England, especially Bristol, with Ayr, Wigtown and Glasgow in Scotland, and with the two towns of St Malo and Morlaix in

Brittany. On the other hand the O'Donnells did not neglect trade with other Irish towns - Galway for example, but also east coast towns such as Drogheda.

Spanish boats are a not unusual sight off the Donegal coast, but few realise how old this trade is, with an agreement formalised in 1556 in the reigns of Queen Elizabeth of England and King Philip of Spain, allowing Spanish boats to fish in the waters off Killybegs and other ports in return for the payment of one thousand pounds per annum. The French, Dutch and Swedes entered into similar agreements in later centuries. Rory O'Donnell, Earl of Tyrconnell, complained in 1607 to King James that the duties on fishing off Killybegs were being denied him, although they had been paid to his ancestors for hundreds of years. Since these duties were worth 500 pounds at the time one can understand his complaint. Ballyshannon, at the other end of Donegal Bay, was the port through which a considerable area was supplied, including Fermanagh and much of Cavan.

In exchange for imports of wine, luxury clothes, and modern weapons and armour, Ballyshannon and other ports traded fish and animal hides. For instance in the case of Bristol, large quantities of salmon were sold by the O'Donnells in return for clothes of the finest quality. This trade is recorded in the English State Papers, and it is clear from these documents that merchants from Bristol knew Tír Chonaill quite well, coming to the county on an annual basis and sometimes staying for a number of months. From the Bretons and the French the O'Donnells bought gun powder, firearms and iron products, as well as wine and salt, in return selling them fish and hides. This was a highly regulated trade with agreements arrived at, signed, and abided by. The O'Donnells themselves had agents living in the Continental ports and from time to time Continental merchants lived in Tír Chonaill itself.

All of this meant that medieval Tír Chonaill was almost independent of the Pale and the rest of Ireland, and, because of its links with Continental Europe, could bypass England as well. On the other hand its commercial links with the lowlands of Scotland and with Brittany and other centres on the Continent gave it a direct contact with some of the leading humanist centres of the day. The O'Donnells were aware of contemporary trends on the continent and built up considerable diplomatic skills.

The three chieftains of the Golden Age - Aodh Rua, Aodh Dubh and Maghnus - were able military men, relying not just on the bravery and numbers of their forces but on careful preparation and the use of tactics. Their military force was not confined to the land but also extended to their fleet of ships, both sea borne and river borne.

As happens in other parts of the world relative prosperity and military and political stability led to a taste for the better things in life. When Aodh

Rua succeeded in beating off the O'Connors of Sligo in 1470 one of the first things he did was to bring back a collection of historic manuscripts including Leabhar na hUidhre and Leabhar Gearr which had been looted from his family in a previous century. It was the same Aodh Rua who was responsible for the fine architecture of Donegal Castle and Donegal Abbey. His son Aodh Dubh shared this interest in ancient Irish manuscripts and in architecture. If trade connected Tír Chonaill with the rest of Europe at the time, so of course did the church; thus we find that Aodh Dubh was in Rome in 1510-1511 when the Sistine Chapel was being completed, and soon after spent more than six months at the English Court, in the company of Henry VIII. It was Maghnus who was responsible for one of the great works of late medieval scholarship in Ireland, the Beatha Choluim Cille, which he wrote before he became chieftain. This trio of O'Donnell chieftains were great patrons of the arts and of the learned classes and during this time the O Cleirighs and the Mac a'Bhairds

came into their own. According to another historian of medieval Ireland, Katherine Simms

"the surplus wealth which the Gaelic Irish chieftains directed entirely towards feasting and poetry corresponded to funds laid out by the ruling classes of other European countries partly on entertainment, but also on magnificent processions, statues, pictures, jewellery and imposing architecture".

Despite their relative independence from the Pale these three chieftains of Tír Chonaill knew that they could not be totally independent, and sought, to one degree or another, to come to the best possible arrangement with the administration in Dublin Castle. This paid off to a large extent. No English army ever set foot in Tír Chonaill during this time, or indeed tried to hinder in any effective way the overlordship of the adjoining area enjoyed by the O'Donnells. It is indeed instructive to remember that at the time of the Renaissance in Europe

Tír Chonaill was ruled by a succession of chieftains who combined innovation, an openness to foreign influences, and a sure political and cultural touch rooted in the native tradition.

There is an old saying that nothing grows in the shade of a big tree; thus the fact that within 50 years of the death of Maghnus O'Donnell it had all come to an end should come as no surprise. The continuing enmity between the descendants of Conall and of Eoghan erupted into battle once more in 1567 when Shane O'Neill attacked the O'Donnells, and advanced into Tír Chonaill. The writing had been on the wall for Gaelic power in Donegal for some decades before it finally ended with the so-called Flight of the Earls in 1607.

In one final attempt by the old order to reverse the tide of English power, an army was organised by Hugh O'Neill, chief of Tír Eoghain, and Red Hugh O'Donnell, beginning a series of battles with the English which came to be known as the Nine Years War. After strenuous efforts on their part the Gaelic chieftains secured a promise of support from the leading continental power of the day, Spain. To meet up with the Spanish expeditionary force, however, O'Neill's and O'Donnell's force had to march the length of the country to Kinsale on the south coast in the depths of the winter of 1601. There over the Christmas-New Year of 1601/1602 they fought and lost the landmark Battle of Kinsale, which brought down the curtain on a political and cultural system that could not compete with that of the neighbouring island. Red Hugh made his way to Spain to try to inject new life into the alliance but died there a little over a year after Kinsale. He was succeeded as Earl of Tyrconnell by his brother Rory, with his cousin Niall Garbh being inaugurated as the last Chieftain of the O'Donnells.

Six years after Kinsale the remaining Gaelic chieftains, recognising that English rule over the country was a fact but unable to bring themselves to accept it, and no doubt knowing what would happen to them if they gave themselves up, decided to leave Ireland for the continent. O'Donnells and O'Neills, and members of other leading families from Ulster and the northern half of the country, including Maguires and Plunketts - in all over one hundred people - took ship in Rathmullan.

This was what was afterwards called the 'Flight of the Earls'. In truth the power of these chieftains had been broken even before Kinsale, and their ability to provide leadership and a measure of prosperity for their people had long gone. They quickly disappeared from history - Rory dying in Rome in 1608 and Hugh O'Neill the following year.

Following the defeat of the O'Donnells no time was lost in dividing up their lands. Donegal Castle was given to Sir Basil Brooke, an officer in the English Army, along with the older castle at Lough Eske and the precincts of Donegal Friary. The castle as one sees it today is in essence Brooke's castle, with only the tower remaining as a link to the O'Donnells. The O'Donnell lands around Ballyshannon were given to Sir Henry Folliott, the captain of the English garrison in the town. Interestingly Lughaidh Ó Cléirigh, the biographer of Aodh Ruadh, was allowed to keep the Ó Cléirigh hereditary lands until 1609, but this was only a short reprieve; "being a mere Irishman and not of English descent or surname" he was dispossessed at the end of that year.

The Brookes, unlike their relations in neighbouring Fermanagh, did not use the grant of land to build a local empire. The Brookes also failed to emulate other major landowners in the county who were to retain their lands until the Land Acts of the late nineteenth century brought an end to the Irish landlord system; the major part of the land in South and Southwest Donegal was held right through the eighteenth and nineteenth centuries by three main families: the

Murray of Broughton, the Conollys and the Conynghams.

One George Murray of Broughton, in Southwest Scotland was one of a group of Scotsmen who received much of the the land in the southwest of the county. By 1618, however, these were forfeit, and the Baronies of Banagh and Boylagh were granted to a relation of his, John Murray from Cockpool, created Earl of Annandale in 1624. The Murray of Broughtons got the land back in the 1660s, after a longrunning and complex legal dispute. The Murray of Broughton or Murray Stewart Estate, between Donegal, Ardara and Killybegs covered large parts of the parishes of Killaghtee, Killymard, Killybegs, Kilcar and Inishkeel, and totalled about 65,000 statute acres.

In addition to the Murray of Broughton Estate there were the Conollys who owned the town and parish of Ballyshannon as well as pockets of land elsewhere in Donegal - east of Donegal Town, part of

Killybegs Town, and the southern part of Sliabh Liag - and in between the Marquis of Conyngham who owned most of the land from Mountcharles and Inver up to the Rosses.

The seventeenth century was a period of great conflict, beginning with the end of the Gaelic order and the O'Donnell power in 1601-1607, and continuing with the wars of 1641-1653, which included the landmark defeat of the last Irish field army at Scariffholis on the banks of the Swilly, and ending with the Williamite Wars. In contrast the eighteenth century was a more settled era, but one can see the beginnings of the crisis of the mid-nineteenth century taking shape in the failure to deal with the population pressures in rural areas, especially the failure to develop towns like Ballyshannon and Donegal Town to take the surplus labour coming off the small farms of Tyrhugh. Some indication of social unrest is evident in the efforts of the United Irishmen in South Donegal. The authorities were sufficiently worried by what was

happening to build a fort in Belleek as a means of controlling movement from Connacht to Ulster. Ballyshannon, through its trade with France, exchanged wool and provisions for wine, brandy, silk, and the ideals of the French Revolution. Although there was no uprising in Donegal, delegates from the county attended provincial meetings of the United Irishmen in numbers, in the years 1797 and 1798.

The mid nineteenth century and subsequent decades saw much social and economic conflict, culminating in the crisis known as the Great Famine, with its unimaginable levels of poverty, hunger and death. This misfortune came as no surprise to anyone in the area who cared to note its developing social problems.

The landowners of South Donegal and to a lesser extent the government had long realised that something needed to be done to improve agricultural practices. To make a start on this endeavour the Tyrhugh Farming Society was formed by a "committee of gentlemen" in November 1800 in the house of a Mrs. Pye in Ballyshannon. Its raison d'etre was to promote "draining land and growing wheat; good enclosures, and quick-set hedges; the improvement and watering of meadow land; the cleanest and neatest farm houses" and so on. In short to make farming in Ireland more like farming in England. Much of the barony of Tirhugh was suitable for the type of agricultural practices hoped for by the gentlemen of the Farming Society; there was one major obstacle however: too many tenants on the land. It would take many decades and the terrible effects of the Great Famine before the numbers of tenants were reduced, albeit in the cruelest possible way.

The good farming land between Donegal Town and Ballyshannon can seem timeless, with its well kept farmsteads and fields enclosed by hedges and dry stone walls. What one sees today, however, dates only from the first half of the nineteenth century, when the rundale system which had

been the norm here, as in other parts of Ireland, was replaced at the insistence of the landlords. The ancient rundale system (from roinn, a share, and dáil, distribute) divided up the land in a townland to the various farming families, with each getting a roughly equal share of fertile tillage land, mountain and bog. The drawback was that this left tenants with unconnected strips of land, and as the population increased and the holdings were further subdivided, farming became increasingly unviable. In Tirhugh the system was already stretched to breaking point before the end of the eighteenth century. When the agriculturist Arthur Young passed through Tirhugh in the late 1770s, he noted the "beautiful landscapes, swelling fields cultivated with the bay flowing up among them", but also that the "partnership" or rundale farms were in a "backward state".

Beginning in 1824 local landowners, including John Hamilton, Colonel Conolly, Rev. Edward Hamilton and Thomas Brooke, led the process which

was intended to replace the rundale system with individual farmhouses and compact farms, and of course fewer tenants. Their chief weapon was the expiration of old leases, which enabled them to replan their estates. By 1855 the process was more or less complete, but the landlords' 'improvements' had by then been completely overshadowed by the effects of the Famine.

In recent years scholars have used the anniversary of the Great Famine of 1845-1850 to undertake new research into the causes of the hunger and its effects. While most of them would agree that the Famine was a disaster waiting to happen, given the overpopulation in rural Ireland and the paucity of efforts to develop modern agriculture, fishing and other industries, discussion continues on the effectiveness or otherwise of the response by the authorities to the greatest calamity this island has seen. Perhaps the most interesting and innovative research has been on the local dimension of the Famine: the extent of the potato blight, and the levels of hunger, disease and mortality varied substantially from county to county, and within counties, from district to district. This was very much the case in south and southwest Donegal, where travellers to the area and local clergy and public officials have left us with accounts of the different conditions prevailing in different parishes.

Long before the Famine struck, the far southwest of Donegal was noted for its poverty and underdevelopment. The Rev. John Ewing, a Church of Ireland Rector whose area included Gleann Cholm Cille, wrote in the 1820s in response to a query from the North West of Ireland Farming Society:

"The food of the inhabitants chiefly potatoes and fish, not much oatmeal. Milk and butter pretty plenty, fuel invariably turf or peat".

From Inishkeel parish, the area around the town of Glenties, John Barrett wrote, also in response to the North West of Ireland Farming Society:

"it is evident that the situation of the inhabitants as to domestic comforts is very bad."

"The general conditions of farmhouses is (sic) bad, that of cottages wretched; the want of cleanliness is the more obvious defect".

Writing in 1835, Lieutenant Lancey of the Ordnance Survey could give a more optimistic account of Donegal parish:

"Although the inhabitants in general cannot boast much wealth, yet their domestic comforts are many."

"The general food of the farming class of inhabitants is potatoes, bread, butter, milk, eggs and fish. Sometimes they have fleshmeat, which is considered a luxury. I have many times witnessed the domestic comforts of the poor farmer's table,

consisting of potatoes, bread, butter and good milk, the bountiful donation of an all gracious God".

The town and port of Ballyshannon, and the surrounding parish, also enjoyed a modicum of prosperity, at least in comparison to the southwest of the county. In the decade before the Famine large amounts of oats, wheat and potatoes were exported from the town; in 1835, for instance, grain exports alone amounted to £11,000. During this period the rental of the local landlord, Edward Connolly, rose from £8,000 to £14,000 per year. The shock which the potato blight brought was perhaps much more intense in those areas which were used to relative prosperity.

The blight reached Donegal soon after its first appearance in Ireland. The Rector of Killaghtee, halfway between Donegal Town and Killybegs, wrote in his diary on the 20th of October 1845

"in an extensive garden in which I have the finest looking potatoes, in

People

good ground, the disease is most lamentably prevalent . . ."

The failure of the potato crop was nothing new; Donegal people had seen it in 1816-1819, in 1821-1822, and in 1830-1831. To make matters worse the herring shoals had deserted the coast from 1822 to 1831, devastating the fishing industry in Killybegs. It quickly became clear that this time the blight was worse than any of the previous crop failures; in the Autumn of 1845 around 50% of the crop was lost. Nevertheless the Great Famine of 1845-1850, terrible as it was, seems to have caused less devastation in southwest Donegal than in some other parts of Ireland. The presence of abundant fishing along the coast, and the strong fishing traditions in Killybegs, Teelin, and other small ports, coupled with the fact that the authorities used Killybegs as their main depot in the Northwest for the distribution of meal, meant that the situation was less calamitous than it might otherwise have been.

The impoverished and starving people of south and southwest Donegal were served by three Poor Law Unions and three workhouses in Glenties, Donegal Town and Ballyshannon, whose catchment population covered much of North Sligo and Leitrim. The workhouse buildings in Ballyshannon are amongst the best preserved of such institutions in Ireland.

It is a curious fact, much commented on in recent writing about the Famine, that there has been, on the part of some at least, a form of collective denial of its effect in their locality. In Gleann Cholm Cille the oral tradition holds that only one local person died during the Famine - reputedly falling from rocks when out gathering seabirds' eggs! In fact the parish lost 17% of its population, through hunger, disease and emigration. Many of those who lived through the terrible times seemed to have pushed it to the back of their minds. The poet William Allingham hardly mentioned the Famine in his diary and letters,

although he was employed as a Customs officer on the coast, and his family were heavily involved in relief work in his native Ballyshannon.

The landlords of the south and southwest come out of the Famine better than many of their compatriots throughout Ireland, or indeed in the north of the county. Few of them, however, could match John Hamilton of Brownhall in the manner in which he earned the respect of his tenants. Hamilton, "this recklessly generous landlord" as a recent biographer calls him, had around 1,200 tenants on his Brownhall lands, a large estate south of Donegal Town on the shores of Donegal Bay, with a further 1,100 on the other side of the Croaghs in Glenfin. The name 'Brownhall' seems to have come from the family's original home of Broomhill in Lanarkshire. The Hamiltons trace their line from Gilbert of Hamildone, and were related by marriage to the Stuarts, the royal line of Scotland.

John Hamilton's concern for his

tenants, from the time he inherited the estate in 1821 until his death in 1884 was well recognised during his life. As early as 1841 Fr. Eugene McCafferty wrote that he hoped "that the Lord may grant you happy and lengthened days here among a people to whom you are and always have been so useful". His successor as parish priest of Donegal and noted opponent of landlordism, Fr. John Doherty, wrote a few years before Hamilton's death that "his many social virtues, the kindliness of his disposition, and the natural warmth and goodness of his nature have endeared him to his tenantry". Hamilton himself claimed that not a single one of his tenants had to go to the Workhouse, and only one died of starvation. Perhaps the most eloquent testimony to how his tenants felt about him is the causeway to St. Ernan's island, where his house was located, built by them as a token of their esteem.

Short of repeating the devastation caused by the Famine and the subsequent mass emigration, some sort of governmental action was needed to provide industry for the surplus labour in the countryside. Governmental action really began to be felt with the setting up of the Congested Districts Board in 1891. The CDB was an agency ahead of its time in many ways, and played a crucial role in rejuvenating Donegal industries like fishing and tweed. The CDB was responsible, amongst other ventures, for promoting the manufacture of Donegal carpets.

While attending the Belfast Horse Show in 1897 a member of the Congested Districts Board, named Wrench, met Alexander Morton, the head of a textile firm based in Darvel in Ayrshire. Morton, born in 1844, had started his working life as a weaver, and built up a business making a variety of textile products, lace chenille and tapestry; machinery woven carpets accounted for a quarter of his sales by the end of the century. He had for some time been thinking about starting up in the business of hand-made high quality carpets, and had

been considering the west of Ireland as a possible base, given the abundance of labour. The meeting with Wrench galvanised him, and having looked at sites in Ardara, Glenties, Cill Chartha (Kilcar) and Gleann Cholm Cille eventually settled on Killybegs. By 1898 the factory was in operation. Morton, an entrepreneur if ever there was one, launched into the business with great enthusiasm, bringing in staff with experience in making Axminster carpets, supervising the building of the factory, and actually investing twice as much in setting up the business as had been agreed with the CDB.

Killybegs carpets were from the first a quality product, made by hand in a process which had been in use for centuries in those countries where the craft had evolved, for example Turkey and Iran. Morton's publicity claimed that Killybegs carpets were "similar in substance to the finest Anatolian carpets"; indeed most of the designs used in the early years were Turkish or Persian in origin. In the factory, built to accommodate up to four hundred workers, the employees, mostly young women, sat side by side in front of woollen warps stretched vertically between two long horizontal rollers. They selected lengths of pre-cut wool, knotting them in the Turkish fashion to the threads of the warp. By the beginning of the new century Morton was using Celtic designs, the first documented example being shown at the Cork Exhibition in 1902, although the firm had made an alter carpet with a Celtic design for the Cathedral in Letterkenny, which opened the previous summer. Donegal or Killybegs carpets earned a great name in the business and continued to be made until after World War II, although the factory was in decline for more than a decade before it was closed in 1954. The business has recently been revived, and high quality hand-made carpets are again being made in Killybegs.

The CDB also devoted much energy to boosting the fishing industry in Killybegs and other ports. During the 1890s a new pier was approved for Killybegs, whose £10,000 cost was borne jointly by the Board and the Treasury. The CDB also invested in new fishing craft and in fish processing. The coming of the railway from Donegal Town west to Killybegs in 1893 meant that there was a much quicker and cheaper way of getting the catch to market.

The art and industry of weaving continues to be associated with the southwest of the county. *Some Irish industries*, published in 1897, includes the memories of "an old Donegal man" who recalled that

"Homespuns have been manufactured in these mountain districts extending from Ardara to Glenhead from time immemorial. In my childhood's days, the peasantry made their own blankets, flannels, etc., principally white and grey, for home wear, and above all they manufactured blue cloth for men's wear.

"I remember seeing the whole street of Ardara lined with hogsheads of flaxseed on fair days during the months of April and May for sale at the monthly fairs. The people then made all their home-made linens for sheets, towels, shirts, etc., and all woven in the district."

The CDB saw weaving - the archetypal cottage industry - as a very suitable means of giving local people in Ardara, Gleann Cholm Cille, An Charraig, and Cill Chartha an income that would keep hunger from the door. Weaving continues to provide income in the area to this day, and Donegal tweed, mostly produced in the area from Donegal Town to Ardara, is one of the county's best known exports.

One of the most remarkable members of the Board was Rev. Patrick O'Donnell, who had become the youngest Catholic bishop of his day when ordained for the See of Raphoe in 1888. O'Donnell was born in Kilraine, not far from Glenties on the road to Ardara. He served on the Board from 1892 until its remit ended with Independence, and amongst other things, ensured that the altar carpet for the new Cathedral in Letterkenny was made by the CDB-assisted factory in Killybegs. He later became Archbishop of Armagh, and a Cardinal. His close relationship with the people of the congested districts of Donegal, most of them Gaelic speakers like him, gave the CDB a measure of credibility in the county which it otherwise might not have had.

The growth of the co-operative movement also contributed to economic renewal. Co-operative creameries were the first to be set up, and they were soon followed by fishing, credit, poultry, home industry and even bee-keeping co-ops. Dairy co-ops were started in Pettigo (1899), Drumholm (1900), Donegal Town (1902), Inver and Ballyshannon (both 1903) and Bruckless (1905), while in the same period co-operative banks were set up in Inver, Killybegs, Lough Eske, Donegal Town, Ballyshannon and Bruckless.

While the condition of the ordinary people of southwest Donegal did improve through the efforts of the CDB and co-ops, it remained harsh. Despite religious emancipation and decades of elementary education through the National Schools their lives, as documented in both the life and writings of Patrick MacGill, 'the Navvy Poet' from Glenties, were marked by poverty and want. MacGill was born on New Year's Day 1891, the eldest of eleven children. After the minimum of formal education, just a few years at the local National School, he was sent to the Hiring Fair in Strabane at the age of twelve, to find work on the more fertile land of Mid-Ulster. Two years later he was on the boat to Scotland, working first as a tatie-hoker in Ayrshire, picking potatoes on the farms there along with hundreds of his fellow Donegal men and women. He soon left that to work as a navvy in the greater Glasgow area, which was then the industrial powerhouse of the British Empire. Unlike many of his compatriots he made up for his lack of formal education by reading in whatever spare time he had. Reading soon inspired writing, and his first book of poems, *Gleanings from a Navvy's Scrapbook*, was published in 1911, when he was just 20.

MacGill never forgot the conditions which first forced him to leave Glenties: the locally powerful and well-connected traders (known as gaimbíní or gombeen-men) whose greed and vindictiveness kept small farmers and labourers in hock inspired much of his writing, most notably, *Children of the Dead End: the autobiography of a Navvy*, published in 1914. *The Rat Pit*, a companion piece to that book which came out in the following year, dealt with the life and harsh existence of Irish migrant labourers in the West of Scotland. If publishing poetry and novels by his early twenties was a remarkable achievement for someone of his background, it did not satisfy MacGill. He first went to London to write for the Daily Express, but unhappy with the life of a journalist he soon moved to Windsor Castle where he found a job as an assistant to the archivist in the Chapter Library. Not surprisingly this caused eyebrows to be raised. When World War I broke out, MacGill enlisted in a London Irish unit of the British Army, an experience which produced two great books from the trenches: *The Great Push* and *The Red Horizon*. Throughout the 1920s he published a stream of novels, mainly inspired by his youth in southwest Donegal. Although he moved to the United States in 1930, his upbringing continued to shape his writing.

A visitor to southwest Donegal will be impressed with the strength of the old traditions and customs in the area - for example the Gaelic language and the Colm Cille turas in Gleann Cholm Cille, and especially the fiddle tradition in the area west of Killybegs and Glenties. The story of fiddle playing in the southwest is above all the story of a number of remarkable families. It is true that the tradition was passed on in a similar way within families elsewhere in Donegal and in Ireland, but in this area - Gleann Cholm Cille, Cill Chartha, Teileann (Teelin) and the surrounding area - it is a really striking feature of music making.

Amongst the leading families were the Cassidys, the Mac Fhionnlaoichs, and the O'Byrnes, better known as the Dearg O'Byrnes or the Deargs. The brothers Johnnie, Frank and Paddy Cassidy came from Cill Chartha, and their cousin Con grew up in nearby Teileann. Of the brothers, Johnnie and Frank were the better regarded players, but all three were well known for house dances. The Cassidys also got involved in promoting dances in a big marquee which they bought as Army surplus in Finner Camp at the end of World War I. Con Cassidy was one of the outstanding fiddlers of the Donegal tradition, a quiet gentle man, blessed with wit, humour and musical genius.

The Mac Fhionnlaoich fiddling family owe their origins to Moses or Mosaí Mac Fhionnlaoich who was born in the beginning of the nineteenth century in Loch Inse, a townland in Gleann Cholm Cille. Mosaí was a blacksmith as well as a fiddle player. Many of his sons also took up the bow, including Maurice Mosaí, who joined the RIC, John Mosaí, and Padaí Mosaí. John Mosaí has left the strongest legacy, with many of his tunes still played today; according to some sources he wrote the local favourite "The Glen road to Carrick". The brothers Mickey Bán and Francie Dearg O'Byrne also founded a dynasty of fiddlers. Their driving rhythmical style was influenced by piping, and they were much in demand, being sought for house dances seven nights a week. Francie Dearg's son Pat and his grandson Peter carry on the tradition and the 'Dearg' style.

The best known fiddling family from Donegal were the Dohertys, a family of travelling fiddlers with their roots in the Gaeltacht Lár around Leitir Mac a'Bháird (Lettermacaward). The Doherty tradition goes back to at least the late 1700s, to Hugh Doherty who played uilleann pipes and warpipes as well as the fiddle. The line passed on through his son Simí Mór and grandson Mickey Mór to the latter's three sons, the famous John, Mickey and Simí Doherty. Donegal fiddle music and indeed the county's cultural heritage owe an awesome debt to these and above all to John or Johnny Doherty. His playing is a link with a Donegal that is no more, a time when folklore and folk beliefs were accepted as facts of life. We have a fair selection of recordings of his playing, and it is fair to say that the fiddlers of the future will continue the path he trod for many years to come. There were many other players besides these leading families, and happily the tradition is at least as strong today as it has ever been, not least due to the efforts of vibrant organisations like Cairdeas na bhFidléirí, and a growing number of fiddling schools and weekends, bringing together musicians and enthusiasts.

The twentieth century is now consigned to history along with the centuries which went before it. While it was not overshadowed by a major cataclysm like the Famine of the nineteenth, or the wars and political and social upheaval of the sixteenth, the twentieth century saw south Donegal struggling to come to terms with the effects of the Border, and the southwest of the county saw continued loss of population. The efforts of the famous Fr., later Canon, James McDyer to turn this trend around in Gleann Cholm Cille have entered the history books. He believed that the future of isolated communities lay in acting for themselves, rather than waiting for central government to come to their rescue. His work is being continued in the glen, through organisations such as Oideas Gael, and the Folk Museum. South Donegal has always been the point where Connacht and Ulster meet, but the creation of a political border between the county and the rest of West Ulster was a profound shock to the area, on a number of levels. Towns like Bundoran, Ballyshannon and Donegal Town found themselves cut off from their hinterland, connected to the rest of the state through a strip of land a mere 7 miles wide. The Border cast a shadow over the economic, social and political life of the south of the county throughout the remainder of the century.

As south and southwest Donegal enters the twenty first century much of what made the area distinctive - its language, pastimes and way of life - are under sustained threat, and visitors from a century ago would be amazed at the changes, most of them in the very recent past. Despite this Donegal retains a recognisable identity, and its people treasure its unique heritage. The new dispensation in Northern Ireland is a source of great hope for towns such as Ballyshannon and Donegal Town, holding out the promise of greater prosperity, along with their neighbours in Fermanagh and West Tyrone. The people of Aodh Ruadh, Adhamnán, Conall and of the O'Donnell chieftains look forward to a brighter future.

Sources

Those readers interested in finding out more about the geology, natural history, culture, and social and economic history of south and southwest Donegal will find the following books useful. Most are still available to buy; the others are available in libraries in Donegal and elsewhere.

Allingham, Hugh. *Ballyshannon: its history and antiquities.* [Ballyshannon: printed by the Donegal Democrat], 1937.

An Charraig=Carrick. An Charraig: Coiste Turasóireachta na Carraige, 1994.

Bernen, Robert. *Tales from the Blue Stacks.* London: Hamilton, 1978.

Bernen, Robert. *The Hills: more tales from the Blue Stacks.* London: Hamilton, 1983

Cnuasach staire & oidhreachta Chill Chartha=A collection of history and heritage of Kilcar. Cill Chartha: Aislann Chill Chartha, 1995.

Conaghan, Charles. *History and antiquities of Killybegs.*[Ballyshannon: printed by the Donegal Democrat], 1975.

Conaghan, Pat. *The Great Famine in South-West Donegal 1845-1850.* Killybegs: Bygones, 1998.

Cunningham, John B. *Lough Derg: legendary pilgrimage.* Monaghan: R & S Printers, 1984.

Day, Angélique, and McWilliams, Patrick. *Ordnance Survey Memoirs of Ireland: Parishes of County Donegal II 1835-6; mid, west and south Donegal.* Belfast: Institute of Irish Studies, QUB, 1997.

Egan, Bernard. *Drumhome.* [Ballyshannon: printed by the Donegal Democrat], 1986.

Gleann Cholm Cille: seoid oidhreachta na hÉireann; treoirleabhar ildaite le léarscáil. Gleann Cholm Cille: Oideas Gael, 1997.

Hart, Henry C. *The Flora of Donegal.* Dublin: Sealy, Bryers and Walker, 1898.

Hoad, Judith. *This is Donegal tweed.* Inver: Shoestring, 1987.

Jennings, Brendan. *Michael O Cleirigh, chief of the Four Masters and his associates.* Dublin: Talbot Press, 1936.

Lacey, Brian and others. *The Archaeology of Donegal.* Lifford: Donegal County Council, 1983.

Leslie, James B. *Raphoe clergy and parishes.* Enniskillen, 1940.

Mac Aoidh, Caoimhín. *Between the jigs and the reels: the Donegal fiddle tradition.* Manorhamilton: Drumlin, 1994.

Mac Congail, Nollaig. *Scríbhneoirí Thír Chonaill.* Dublin: FNT, 1983.

McGill, Lochlann. *In Conall's footsteps.* Dingle: Brandon, 1992.

McGinley, T.C. (i.e. 'Kinnfalea'). *The Cliff scenery of South-Western Donegal.* Derry: [Derry Journal], 1867.

Maguire, Edward. *Ballyshannon: past and present.* Bundoran: Stephens, [193-].

Maguire, Edward. *A History of the Diocese of Raphoe.* Dublin, 1920. 2 vols.

Marsden, John. *The Illustrated Columcille.* London: Macmillan, 1991.

Micks, William L. *An Account of the Congested Districts Board for Ireland.* Dublin: Eason, 1925.

Murphy, Desmond. *Derry, Donegal and modern Ulster 1790-1921.* Derry: Aileach Press, 1981.

Nolan, William, Ronayne, Liam, and Dunlevy, Mairead. *Donegal: history and society; interdisciplinary essays on the history of an Irish county.* Dublin: Geography Publications, 1995.

O'Donnell, Michael. *'In-through people'.* Letterkenny: Donegal Printing, 1996.

O'Donnell, Terence. *Franciscan Donegal.* Ros Nuala: the Friary, 1952.

O'Hanrahan, Brenda. *Donegal authors: a bibliography.* Dublin: Irish Academic Press, 1982.

Ó hEochaidh, Seán. *Síscéalta ó Thír Chonaill=Fairy legends from Donegal.* Dublin: Comhairle Béaloideas Éireann, 1977.

Patterson, W. J. *Rossnowlagh remembered.* [Ballyshannon: printed by the Donegal Democrat], 1991.

Pitcher, W. S. and Berger, A. R. *The Geology of Donegal.* New York: Wiley-Interscience, 1972.

Purcell, Deirdre. *On Lough Derg.* Dublin: Veritas, 1988.

Rowan, Alistair. *North West Ireland.* London: Penguin, 1979. [Buildings of Ireland series].

Shanklin, Eugenia. *Donegal's changing traditions: an ethnographic study.* New York: Gordon and Breach, 1985.

Silke, John J. *Two abbots.* Letterkenny: Diocese of Raphoe, 1997.

Sheppard, Liz. *Donegal for all seasons.* Ballyshannon: Donegal Democrat, [198-].

Trimble, T.H. (Harry). *Historical meanderings around Lough Eske.*[Letterkenny: printed by Browne (Printers)], 1996.

Dear Reader

We hope you have enjoyed this book. It is one of a range of illustrated titles which we publish. Other areas currently featured include:–

Strangford Shores
Dundalk & North Louth
Armagh
Belfast
Antrim, town & country
Inishowen

Donegal Highlands
Drogheda & the Boyne Valley
The Mournes
Fermanagh
Omagh
Ballynahinch and the Heart of Down

Cottage Publications
15 Ballyhay Road
Donaghadee, Co. Down
N. Ireland, BT21 0NG

Also available in our 'Illustrated History & Companion' Range are:-

Coleraine and the Causeway Coast
Lisburn
Ballymoney

City of Derry
Banbridge
Holywood

We can also supply prints, individually signed by the artist, of the paintings featured in the above titles as well as many other areas of Ireland.

For the more athletically inclined we can supply the following books from our illustrated walking book series:-

Bernard Davey's Mournes

Tony McAuley's Glens

For more details on these superb publications and to view samples of the paintings they contain, you can visit our web site at **www.cottage-publications.com** or alternatively you can contact us as follows:-

Telephone: +44 (028) 9188 8033

Fax: +44 (028) 9188 8063